Other books by Dr. Philip S. Berg

Kabbalah for the Layman
Reincarnation: The Wheels of a Soul
The Kabbalah Connection
Power of the Aleph Beth

As Editor

An Entrance to the Tree of Life
An Entrance to the Zohar
A Study of Ten Luminous Emanations, Volume II

As Translator

The Zohar

Available from your bookseller or
RESEARCH CENTRE OF KABBALAH INTERNATIONAL
200 PARK AVENUE, NEW YORK, N.Y. 10017

ASTROLOGY
AThe Star
Connection

Dr. Philip S. Berg

RESEARCH CENTRE OF KABBALAH INTERNATIONAL

NEW YORK • PARIS • JERUSALEM

Designed by T.H. Richards/ILNY Communications and Media Corp.

Jacket design by Osnat Youdkevich

FIRST EDITION
August 1986

ISBN 0-943688-36-1 (Hardcover)
0-943-688-37-X (Softcover)

For further information, address:
RESEARCH CENTRE OF KABBALAH
200 PARK AVENUE, SUITE 303E
NEW YORK, N.Y. 10017
— OR —
RESEARCH CENTRE OF KABBALAH
P.O. BOX 14168
THE OLD CITY, JERUSALEM
ISRAEL

PRINTED IN U.S.A.

To Karen, a beautiful Libra,
for hastening
the final redemption of
The Age of Aquarius.

ASTROLOGY
The Star
Connection

In Love and Memory of My Dear Mother
Sarah Bat Mordechai
of Blessed Memory,
who passed into the Eternal World
on June 21, 1978.

— MERRELL WARSHAW

My greatest debt for the writing of *The Star Connection* is owed to Kenneth R. Clark, editor at the *Chicago Tribune*, for compiling, reviewing, and editing the manuscript, and for his writing of the preface.

He made fundamental and frequent contributions to the essential ideas and their connection to the overall style. The light I found in our many discussions is one of my principal rewards from this book.

— *Dr. Philip R. Berg*
August, 1986
New York City

About The Author

Philip S. Berg was born in New York City. An ordained Rabbi who holds a doctorate in comparative religion, when travelling to Israel in 1962 met his kabbalistic master Rabbi Yehuda Z. Brandwein, then dean of the Research Centre of Kabbalah. During that period the Centre expanded substantially with the establishment of the United States branch in 1965 through which it disseminates and distributes its publications. Berg did research at the Centre, writing five books on such topics as creation, energy, cosmic consciousness and the origins of Kabbalah. Following the death of his master in 1969, Berg assumed the position of dean of the Centre, expanding its publication program through translation of source material on the Kabbalah into other languages. Berg moved to Israel with his wife Karen in 1971 where they began to feel deep stirrings for the majority of Jews alienated from their roots. They then opened the doors of the Centre to all seekers of self-identity, establishing centres in all major cities throughout Israel, while at the same time lecturing at the City University of Tel Aviv. They returned to the United States in 1981.

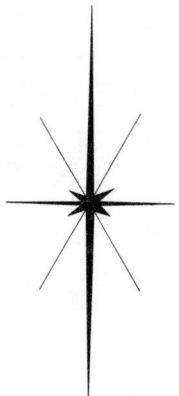

Contents

Chapter 2: Desire — A Key to the Cosmos   13

Systems of transfer; Differences in intelligence; Spirituality; Gravity; Information; Inner consciousness; Pure frequency; Extinction of the dinosaurs; Multiple levels of parallel universe; Time travel and the speed of light; Restriction and free will; The crude spirit realm; Addressing catastrophe and other life-threatening situations; As above so below; The steady rhythm of the universe; Idol worship; Mind control; Interplanetary communication; Cosmic battle; Star wars; Cataclysm; Aquarian influence

Chapter 3: Astral Influence — Gamble or Guarantee?   37

Astral influences; Signs of the Zodiac; The four elements; Astral entities; Destiny; The Zero election year; The bizarre Lincoln-Kennedy Coincidence; Quantum mechanics; Cause and effect; The mind element; Uncertainty; Roboticized technology; Predeterminism or free will; The Moon influence; Eclipse; The sun and moon; Day and night; Extraterrestrial intelligence; Cosmic nerve centers

Chapter 4: Cosmic Wanderers   59

Comets; Omens of disaster; Rebellious member of the solar system; Origin of comets; The unified circuitry of energy

Chapter 5: Beyond the Test Tube   63

Pure science and the religionist; Signals from extraterrestrial sources; Medieval absolutism; Cosmic container; The planetary influence; Changing destiny; Stars impel not compel; As above so below; Death as a transition period; The four basic realities; The levels of consciousness; Cosmos: Past, present and future; Expanding consciousness of Moses; Cosmic energy capsules

Chapter 6: What's in a name?   83

Blind destiny and free will; Fear of the unknown; Destiny in the stars; Rewriting destiny; The Lord as an intimate concept; The chart of destiny; The universal law of tikune; The interface and lineup of astral bodies; The metaphysical interface; The destiny pattern; The reincarnation process; The spiritual lifestyle; The cargo of tikune; The software; Soul baggage; Chains of predestination; The oppurtunity in a single moment; Predictable destiny as opposed to free will; Parallel levels; The universal travel through time; Cosmic consciousness; Manipulating fate; Power of R. Shimon Bar Yohai; Destiny of the world; Cosmic computer

Preface

ANEWSPAPER EDITOR LAYING OUT HIS DAILY EDITION CAN OMIT the story of the year from page one and few, if any, of his readers will notice, but let him inadvertently drop the astrology column from its accustomed place back by the funny papers and they will jam his switchboard with their outrage.

Prosperous young urban professionals with MBAs from Harvard and stock portfolios from Wall Street strike up conversations with strangers with the oldest line in the lexicon of the lonely: "Hi there, what's your sign?" In the publishing industry, astrology long has been a "hot property," mining millions every year by offering sun signs for everything from lovers to pets. Americans, always wary of being taken for fools, scoff at astrology and make jokes about it, yet pursue it as if as it were the breath of life.

What they are getting, however, from that daily newspaper column over which they will threaten a careless editor with mayhem is little more than they would get from a Chinese fortune cookie.

"Romance looks highly promising," one such column recently advised all Sagittarians. Leos were warned that "Travel could be hectic."

Even the best of books on conventional astrology offer only half the picture. Sun signs, rising signs, moon signs and the casting of individual horoscopes are important, but they are the result, not the cause, where astrology is concerned. This is not a book about conventional astrology. This is a book about Kabbalistic astrology which is the oldest and wisest application of the science known to mankind, and since the Kabbalist always asks the question, "Why?" no rising signs or horoscopes are presented here. They will be covered in a subsequent book, after the "why" of astrology has been answered, and it is answered here in terms of origins, concepts, cosmic connections and the debate between free will and determinism. This pathway to astrology stretches all the way back to Father Abraham and leads beyond the stars, into worlds devoid of time, space motion where physics and metaphysics become one. This is a book about power and wisdom and the tapping of energies and intelligences beyond the wildest imaginings of those who know what the Zodiac is without ever asking how it got that way or where it came from.

This is the way of Kabbalah among the constellations. Welcome to its journey.

— *Kenneth R. Clark*

Introduction

"The heavens declare the glory of the creator, the expanse of the sky tells of His handiwork. Day following day brings expression of praise and night following night bespeaks wisdom." [1]

E VER SINCE MY ENTRY INTO THE WORLD OF JEWISH MYSTICISM, I have been interested in astrology, sensing that there is more to it than what the conventional astrology books provide. What, to me, seemed most disturbing, was the severe dichotomy between science, astronomy and Western culture on the one hand, and the esoteric dimension of astrology, with its potential influence upon our universe and the individual on the other. I was deeply disappointed by the quality of research and scientific approach in the writing of most astrologers.

When widespread disillusionment with the scientific community began to take hold during the early 1970s, one field of scientific endeavor remained unscathed. The science of the heavens, astronomy, with the cosmic soul connection that unquestionably had its origins in the remote past, remains for us today as potent a symbol as ever for the wider explanation of scientific endeavor.

The compulsive fascination with exploration of the unknown out there in our universe has existed within man as long as he could observe the structure and order of the cosmos. This preoccupation with the cosmic connection arose when a fundamental awareness of the enormous and profound dimensions of the celestial realm and its powerful influence over the affairs of man became firmly established. Astronomy always held a significance for us beyond the simple matter or navigation.

The ancient worship of planetary bodies in the heavens, the mystical astrologer whose interpretation of cosmic influence and their relationship to man's destiny and future, testify to the remote and ancient past of the science of astronomy. Further developments in technology providing a deluge of information concerning cosmic systems has shown that the universe is far more bewildering and complex than heretofore was suspected. It is clear and beyond any doubt that our understanding of the celestial world beyond the sky still is in its infancy, and the exact nature of man and his relationship to our vast universe is as yet only dimly perceived.

Since time immemorial, people have been moved by the unfolding panorama provided by ancient astronomers and astrologers, yet with each new discovery, the information seemed more confusing and baffling, creating more mysteries and questions than solutions. In spite of the enormous and rapid social progress that can be attributed to high technology, most people feel that scientific values threaten their very existence. When some physicists regard the singularity, in which a star can collapse without limit until it has shrunk away to an overpowering invisibility, as the end of space and time, we are gradually drawing close to the disintegration of the known laws of nature. Taken all together, the social as well as the scientific implications, we then should be searching for the interface between the supernatural and the natural; the bridge between the known and the unknown.

When I was led to the ancient and first known work on the Kabbalah, the "Sefer Yetzira" (The Book of Formation), authored by the Patriarch Abraham, I realized that I had indeed found the missing link; a connection that would provide a vast realm of potential wisdom of astrology in all its deeper ramifications and importance for us today. This book will not dwell upon rising signs, moon signs, natal charts or character traits and future prospects ascribed to the Taurus, the Virgo or the Sagittarian. Much of this singular preoccupation is little more than a parlor game or a conversation starter and is best left to pop astrology books and daily newspaper columns. This book rather will provide an in-depth study and profound penetration into the fields of extra-terrestrial intelligences, interplanetary relationships, astronomy and cosmic energy fields that will eventually blow away the skepticism of many people in western society. In that sense, this book will be less a book on astrology as the average layman views it than a study of the subject as it was interpreted by the Kabbalist in his search for the ultimate meaning of cosmos and its application to human life on this fleeting terrestrial plane. In that regard, what struck me most as I began my study, was the cosmic language of which these Kabbalists made use, and more importantly, the methodology that enabled them to use the Kabbalah to perceive the essential reality. This would provide them with answers as to how and why these intelligences began, along with their internal cosmic structures.

All of these factors, taken together, eventually led me to the essential values and truths of simplicity that ultimately removed the veil of occultism that surrounded the study of astrology. Einstein said, "All knowledge about reality begins with experience and terminates with it."[2] Consequently, the discovery of anything new beyond the obvious structure as we all see it must invite trouble in any attempt to persuade others to perceive things through lenses other than our own. Who, then, is to determine what is real or unreal concerning our planetary system. And how is he to do it? When most space conclusions are based on the evolutionary theory of the "Big Bang,"[3] one then must question the validity of these conclusions in their entirety, especially since the primary and essential question as the reason for the Big Bang never has been accurately determined.

From everything we have learned about astrophysics in the intervening half century, we still do not have answers to some simple questions, foremost of which is, what really took place immediately prior to, during, and after the Big Bang?

There is, in fact, only one course that should be pursued. We must return to the moment of the Big Bang for a rendezvous with the cosmic intelligence that was there. We can do that by connecting with credible Kabbalists who made just such a trip and returned from an encounter with the Big Bang by way of the ultimate trip in mystical time travel. While time travel, according to the physicists, is beyond our present capabilities, traveling backward in time has existed for those who were steeped in the knowledge of Kabbalah.

The traditional notions of space and time, once noted as separate and distinct entities, became inextricably linked by Einstein's theory of relativity. Subsequently, they were recognized by scientists as a fourth dimension of our universe with the realization that one can move through time just as we move through space. Relativity has taken us beyond our consciousness and experience and normal reasoning seems to become obsolete.

We are told by our scientists that if one could travel faster than the speed of light, time actually would proceed into the past. An astronaut, capable by some means as yet unknown to physical science of exceeding the speed of light, possibly could zoom into deep space and return before he left — a thought that once never could have been accepted in the scientific community and which certainly has lain beyond the comprehension of the layman.

When a scientist begins talking about an elastic time that can be extended or reduced, stretched or shrunk, places where time no longer exists or where subatomic particles travel back in time, established laws of science must be reconsidered. Though such forms of time may appear to be unacceptable to most of us, it nevertheless opens the doors to even more, and stranger, phenomena and seems to challenge our most rigid laws and principles of logic. Mathematical formulae suggest two-way time travel, yet, for the most part, the paradoxical consequences keep it within the framework of science fiction.

The most common flaw presented against the concept of two-way time travel has become known as "the Grandfather Paradox." A time traveler would encounter it if he returned to the past just in time to prevent the meeting of his grandparents, which means that he, himself, never was born. But had he not been born, he could not have prevented the meeting of his grandparents or have been present to go back in time in the first place. Yet, from the world view of the Kabbalist[4], there is nothing paradoxical about such a trip, simply because a time traveler undertaking it would prevent the meeting of his grandparents, not in the universe to which he was born, but in a parallel universe in which he never existed prior to or after his one invasive junket.

This imaginary paradox, however, is little more than a child's puzzle compared with some of the real ones that now confront the physicist. One of them might very well spell the breakdown of the presently conceived laws of nature or even the end of the world for science. It is the discovery, in mathematical terms at least, of spacetime naked singularities, or black holes, which come about as a result of the gravitational collapse of giant stars. Black holes hold bizarre properties. Absolutely nothing, not even light, can escape their immense gravity. Even the original intelligence that produced the black hole in the first place is trapped within it. It is exactly at this point that gaps in our understanding of the workings of the physical world have arisen. The image of our physical world is one of a complex web of influences, closely interwoven, continually acting and reacting between its integral parts.

Inasmuch as man is internally fragmented, only a fragment of the total picture can be understood. Yet there is common acceptance that everything that is happening in our universe is entirely dependent upon and determined by everything else. Along with the threat of a naked singularity, our frail minds must face the chaos of our universe. Many scientists today believe that the entire cosmos is slowly disintegrating, just as are the organized structures we call our bodies. Just as people grow old and die and mountains are washed away, the ultimate stage of stellar depletion of energy is the black hole with which nothing survives an encounter. When an object falls into a black hole, all form, intelligence and identity are wiped out forever. This rather depressing conclusion about the inevitability of entropy has led many scientists to assume that the entire universe eventually will become nothing more than a burned-out cosmic clinker.

What then is the purpose of these celestial bodies? How and why did they begin? Without some answers to these fundamental questions, we never can face up to the ultimate unknowable future. Rather, we must take our chances on whatever the universe throws at us. Any attempt, and there have been many scientific attempts in the past 300 years, to explain and describe the enormously arranged and beautifully designed universe we now inhabit with information based upon events that occurred after the Big Bang leaves all conclusions hanging on a thread. Scientists still cling to the belief that understanding our cosmos lies not in the original initiation of its beginning, structure and organization, but upon understanding the laws and principles of nature that maintain the cosmic system and force it to operate in an orderly fashion. To ignore the issue of causality, and more importantly, the purpose behind each cause and effect simply because this issue is very complex and subtle, appears to be a cheap way out for physics. Probability, which still plays a large part in subatomic physics, fails to cope adequately with the physics which lie beyond gravitational collapse. Such an uncertainty well might spell the end of the road for physics as an exact science. I am sure that as we probe nature more deeply, we will uncover a whole new era in physics — one more basic and more beautiful. This seems to be the expectation of John Wheeler, the famous astrophysicist, who wrote, "Some day a door will surely open and expose the glittering central mechanism of the world in its beauty and simplicity. Toward the arrival of that day, no development holds out more hope than the paradox of gravitational collapse."[5]

The path to this new age of physics, which lies beyond the boundaries of infinity where the limits of lightspeed cease to exist, already is provided by the Zohar. Shimon Bar Yohai, in his "Book of Splendor," realized that in order to face the unknowable, it would be necessary to discover the cause of these events — an undertaking that presents a difficulty with which contemporary physics cannot cope. It is precisely this encounter with the unknowable about which a few scientists already declare will remain forever beyond the domain of intellectual inquiry. Yet ancient Kabbalists held the key, as the following Zohar will indicate:

"R. Elazar and R. Abba were sitting together one evening and when it grew dusk they went to a garden by the Sea of Kinneret. As they were going, they saw two stars rush towards each other from different points in the sky, meet, and than disappear. Said R. Abba, 'How mighty are the works of the Creator, the primordial cause, both in heaven above and in the earth below! Who can understand it, these two stars emerging from different directions, then meeting and disappearing?' R. Elazar replied, 'Did we not see them? We reflected upon them as on many other great works which the Creator is constantly performing.'"

While a complete description of stars in general and their function in particular is beyond the scope of this introduction, several points within this very abstruse Zohar are worth noting.

"There are, in the Kabbalistic view, principally two types of stars. The internal intelligence structure of stars resembles principally the electron. The basic property of stars, their mass or energy charge, originates from and consists of one of three primary negative intelligent forces, including male and female negative energy forces. Stars themselves act as an extension of these energy charges. A star which makes manifest the female negative energy force is drawn from the southern cosmic energy field referred to as the right, or positive, column. A star which manifests the male negative energy force draws its internal intelligence composite from the northern cosmic energy field referred to as the left, or negative, column."[6]

This is the explanation for the cosmic meeting of the two celestial bodies mentioned in the foregoing Zohar. One structure was of a male negative intelligence and the other was a female negative intelligence force. When they were drawn to each other, they nullified each other, shrinking and returning to their unmanifested state of pure intelligence waiting to become manifest again. Their return to the original past state is accomplished through time travel exceeding the speed of light and running off again to infinity waiting for its intelligence to make its next move. This scenario, expressed in meta-physical, rather than physical, terms, sounds like one drawn from a science fiction drama, but we are provided by the account by two noted Kabbalists for whom time travel back to the past did not appear to be a problem. The reply of R. Elazar, "Did we not see them? For we reflected upon them as on many other great works," indicates that they could recognize and qualify the internal structure of these celestial bodies. For them, facing the infinite did not prove to be a harrowing experience, nor, for that matter, did facing a world that abounds with infinity.

Another point worth noting is that in nature there is no inherent uncertainty or unpredictability that becomes manifest. Nor should positions of energy forces be envisaged as roaming around in a random sort of way. It is our inability to define and recognize the various entities of intelligence at the subatomic, or celestial, level that bars us from well defined concepts. R. Elazar, who achieved a higher degree of an altered state of consciousness, found no difficulty in defining precisely what was taking place. He then could tap information that made the absolute future and the past very distinct realities. Taken altogether, and assuming we are ready for the new age of infinity, how does one go about gathering this new kind of information?

The author of the Zohar envisaged this epoch-making Aquarian period by providing some of the knowledge that now has become necessary:

"For there is not a concept or aspect within the human body which does not have its counterpart in the world as a whole. For a man's body consists of varying degrees of concepts and aspects, all acting and reacting upon each other so as to form one organism. So does the world at large consist of a hierarchy of created things which, when they properly act and react upon each other, together form literally one organic body."[7]

What seems to emerge from the Zohar is a phenomenon best described as parallel and interrelated, yet independent, worlds or universes. They are composed of an endless number of universe tracks that will ultimately reflect different patterns and outcomes of each of the lives of an individual. We might crudely compare this phenomenal concept to our present day computer systems which may include many varied programs within their software.

The frames of reference concerning the limiting speed of light barrier deal more specifically with the physical world as we see it. Reality, as observed by the Kabbalist, is composed of infinite figures of metaphysical references where time or the speed of light barrier cease to exist. Synchronous events long have been attacked by the scientific community as "mere coincidence" if ever they come in conflict with the limiting aspect of the lightspeed barrier, yet according to Einstein's theory of relativity, any influence between particles must require an energy transfer and that energy cannot move instantaneously. Energy can move only at the speed of light or less. The Zohar[8] suggests that the quantum physics theory is correct, but the Zohar also states[9] that there is a never-ending contact that continues to influence other events no matter how far apart they seem to be from each other. According to the Zohar, space communication can take place instantaneously across the universe. When we fail to observe this phenomenon, the inability lies within the vessel's limited capability to reveal it. The instant contact, which exceeds the speed of light, already has taken place.

From a Kabbalistic viewpoint, matters of metaphysics should and could be validated. Recall the urging of Rabbi Shimon Bar Yohai that the concepts of metaphysics be considered on the basis that such concepts could, in some form, be validated by manifestations and physical expressions.

By the path of Kabbalah, we can gain an insight into the *whys* of the entire spectrum of astronomy where the scientist has found barriers he still is unable to penetrate. Through the knowledge of revealment, Kabbalistic astrology, in penetrating these inner sanctums, provides plausible explanations for the movements of solar activity. We thus have taken a giant step forward in bridging the gap and providing the necessary link between celestial and terrestrial entities. How do we really know, from a Biblical viewpoint, that astral influence does exist? Several parts of the Bible, once decodified, will provide the answer.

"And the Lord made two great lights. The greater light to rule the

day and the lesser light to rule the night. He made the stars also and to
rule over the day and night and to divide the light from the darkness.
And the evening and morning were the fourth day."[10]

Just how involved is the Bible with the heavenly bodies? It is no ex-
aggeration to say that the Bible is freighted with material dealing with
the heavens. By the words "to rule," the Bible means to manifest or to
dominate. The sun and the moon, specifically referred to in the
foregoing verse, are cited as "ruling" bodies. So from the first Biblical
verse in the days of creation, we are given our first Biblical support of
astrology as a discipline of importance. The seven days of creation,
from a Zoharic standpoint, are more specifically related to the seven
"planets" of astrology as "rulers" of our galaxy. The beauty of why
there are seven planets in the discipline of astrology, rather than eight
or nine, will be more fully discussed in a later chapter.

Another indication of the importance of astral influences and their
composite is revealed in the "Book of Splendor" and the "Book of Formation" concernign what might appear to be a very unimportant part
of the Bible, namely, Jacob and his 12 sons.[11] The Zohar asks of what
importance the Bible assigns to the fact that Jacob had 12 sons, rather
than 11 or 13. Those who compiled the Bible considered astrology to
be the hand of the Creator written boldly across the heavens. It is
natural for the Bible to reveal the spiritual, or metaphysical, ruler-
ships, noting again the words "to rule," by matching the 12 sons of
Jacob to the 12 constellations to which they correspond.

The Bible takes great pains to elaborate how each name of the 12
sons was chosen. In effect, from a Kabbalistic viewpoint, this reflects
the astrology of Judaism by having each son of Jacob assigned the
spiritual, metaphysical, rulership of the constellations. The story of
Jacob and his 12 sons is the genesis of the Jewish people and it evolved
accordingly. Those who believe the study of astrology to be foreign to
Judaism first would have to reconcile the elaborate Biblical tale that
goes to great lengths in describing the births and the rationale behind
the names of each of the 12 sons of Jacob. If this were not of supreme
importance, it does not seem conceivable that the Bible would devote
such a great amount of ink to the story.

Another important reference in which the Zohar has an extensive interpretation is Numbers which says, "Everyman of the children of Israel shall pitch by his own standard with the ensign of their fathers' house, and on the east side toward the rising of the sun shall they of the standard of the camp of Judah pitch their armies." The pasasage is continued in verse 10, which says "and on the south side shall be the standard of the camp of Reuben, according to their armies. . .along with Judah, thou shalt pitch next to him (on the east side) there shall be the tribe of Issachar and the tribe of Zebulun. . .And on the south side, and those which pitch by him shall be the the tribe of Simeon on the side of Reuben, and also the tribe of Gad."

Thus do we have three tribes on the east side, three on the south side,and on the west, the standard of the camp of Ephriam, Manassah, and Benjamin, "And then the standard of the camp of Dan shall be on the north side, and those that encamp by him shall be the tribe of Asher and Naphtali,"[12] corresponding to right, left and central columns and representing the original "elements" of earth, air, fire and water. Each tribe understood the power of cosmos and their flags became and controlled the 12 signs of the Zodiac.

This passage, seemingly abstruse to the casual reader, actually describes the body of knowledge that is the totality of astrology. It is one of many coded passages in the Bible and it means, simply, that by the power of God, given to the Israelites in the Great Exodus, people from that day forward would have control over their own lives should they desire to exercise it.

The key word here is "sign." It corresponds to the verse in Genesis,[13] "Let there be lights in the firmament of the heavens to divide the day from the night, and let them be for signs and for seasons, and for days and years." Again, the "sign" is a reference to the signs of the Zodiac—Jacob's sons—which were potentially created on the fourth day along with all of the other planets.

From such seed, planted at once in the wilderness of Sinai and in the heavens above it, did the Kabbalistic view of astrology grow. Let us then examine it, root, trunk, branch and leaf, and learn that it holds far more than the traits and alleged fortunes of sun signs offered in daily newspapers.

ASTROLOGY
The Star Connection

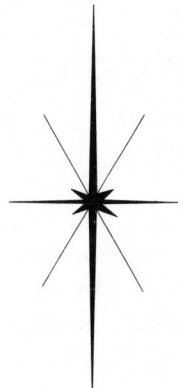

1

A Search for Credentials

"A fool sees not the same tree that a wise man sees."
— William Blake, *A Memorable Fancy*

ONE OF THE PRINCIPAL ARGUMENTS AGAINST ASTRAL INfluences relies on the assumption that the science of astrology is either completely unknown or totally increadible. The usual question is: "How can planets possibly influence our day-to-day affairs on this earth?"

Examine this question closely and you will see that it is a premise that would make it possible to understand a causal relationship between distant objects not physically or otherwise linked. It is like saying that what the eye does not see and what the ear does not hear simply does not exist, yet this could be the most valid argument in support of, or in challenge against, astrology. In astrology, what one believes or, does not believe is an important matter. The other sciences can be verified by experiment and consequently are subject to the workings of the laws and principals of science. Astrology has developed from pure metaphysics and cannot be verified as a physical science.

A physicist, to make the point even stronger, will say that the universe is composed of a vast number of particles of matter in electromagnetic fields and any events or changes that may take place result from the impact of one force (or particle) upon another. It is this notion of causality—that one particle has caused another to move—that the whole framework of science as we know it today is based. In astrology, however, this causal relationship between two objects is separated by immense gulfs of empty space not unlike that which stretches between the earth and the moon.

Experts love to classify astrology as an unscientific system somewhere between past time and the occult—superstitious and mystical. Its sister science, astronomy, was recognized as a real science only after Copernicus proved that the earth, far from being the center of the universe, was merely one tiny part of an entire solar complex. Through telescopic astronomy, it was revealed that the individual members of the solar system obeyed mysterious but exact laws and principals. Astrology, on the other hand, cannot meet this requirement. The most that one might expect in the validation of astrology is that there seems to be some evidence that it works. The question of why it works, up until the publication of this book, has been an unfair one. There is no physicist or scientist in any particular discipline who can explain why things work the way they do. Physics is called physics because it basically attempts to explain what is, rather than provide some plausible explanation of why it is. This book will attempt to validate the study of astrology by explaining the why of solar and lunar activity, planetary motion and seasonal shift through the affect they have upon those who live under their influence.

The composition and structure of planetary forces have eluded all of our space explorations. The surface, gravitational and magnetic fields of celestial bodies are of a nature that defies direct contact even by the most advanced spacecraft. Science therefore is able to provide us with very little in the way of definitive information. Man landed on the moon and returned with samples of the rocks that litter its surface but none of this activity has provided us with the overall answers that we seek. Man has one very serious handicap. He cannot always see that at which he is looking, especially on the surface of the moon which is an entirely different frame of reference for his limited mind. He is insulated from it by a space suit, boots and a canned and compressed earth atmosphere. Even the data he relays back to earth by telemetry is subject to a host of unknown forces that can distort meaning. We have enough trouble observing our environment right here on earth where we were bred, born and reared.

It happens all the time, right here on our own, familiar terrestrial level. We have difficulty really observing things that we see. We come to trust our five senses and along comes Heisenberg to tell us that we must apply the uncertainty principle to everything because the things with which we do come in direct contact present so many problems that we stand on the brink of no reality! There are no such things as absoluteness. Heisenberg demonstrated that physical behavior of nature confirms the quantum theory's schizophrenic description of subatomic conduct in the most daring way possible.

Nature continues to draw a curtain across its face whenever scientists attempt to obtain information that seems inconsistent with quantum mechanics. Heisenberg's injection of the uncertainty principle rules out the possiblity of anyone ever performing the measurements needed to define any physical idea, leaving us with no precise definition of the real or even the unreal. Philosophers have struggled with the problem for years, but only in recent years have we begun to hear it from the physicists who are in more of a dilemma because the more technology is advanced, the further they are taken from reality.

What one does not "know" is that with which one has not come in contact. Adam "knew"[14] Eve and she conceived and bore Cain. How can the mere act of knowing create a pregnancy? The Zohar explains this simply as the difference between information and knowledge. Knowing is the connection. Obviously there was an act of physical intercourse, but that is not the point sought by the Zohar which cites this particular verse in Genesis to illustrate that the only time information becomes knowledge is when direct contact has been made with the information sought. Direct contact, as opposed to mere awareness that something is there, even on a metaphysical level alone yields knowledge. Since man, still imprisoned in other frames of reference, including space suits and a canned atmosphere, never really has touched the moon, he really can have no knowledge of it even when the information he sends back to earth via telemetry may fill volumes.

There are no such things as unrelated, completely independent entities in this universe. Consequently, anything received back on earth from a space probe must be questioned as to accuracy because it can be so distorted under the new theory of quantum physics or, for that matter metaphysical influences originations from other areas of cosmos.

Any maker of microchips will be able to explain the frustration that quantum mechanics imposes upon the necessary process of locating a single electron by means of the electron microscope. The microscope uses a stream of electrons to make its measurements, and by the time the electron sought is "found," the electron stream being used in the probe has moved it and it isn't there any more. In short, the very act of observing changes that which is observed, forcing microchip makers to play blind statistical odds in the creation of their tiny miracles. The observational problems, however, exist on the macrocosmic, as well as the microcosmic, plane.

Astronomers initially thought Saturn boasted only six rings, but telemetry received from recent robot probes has indicated that there are more than 1,000, and what may appear to be no more than haphazard "noise" within those rings may be more closely related to intelligence, and no matter how closely we monitor intelligence, by the time we connect with it, it already has undergone enormous changes because of the principles of quantum mechanics. Thus, establishing any conclusion, which is to say "knowledge," must, of necessity, include enormous uncertainty. What, then, is "real?" The poor physicist stumbles on, using his very limited base of knowledge, and refuses to come to grips with what actually has become reality, whatever it may have been when he first went searching for it. How does he reconcile his work with Einstein's theories inasmuch as it was only within Einstein's frame of reference that energy can move only at the speed of light or less? What of influence on a physical basis, or, more importantly, at the metal level, where synchronous events take place seemingly with no mutual connection?

According to the Zohar, quantum physics is not merely operative on the physical plane. The Zohar states that, "Man is an exact replica, an exact duplicate, of the universe as a whole," meaning that events occurring within the human body are doing so with energy transfers far greater than the speed of light.

From a Kabbalistic point of view, light has no "speed" whatsoever.[15] To the Kabbalist, light is ever present and pervades the universe, even though we lack the ability to see it. When a mechanism, or vessel, such as a light bulb actually reveals light for us that is there in the first place, we erroneously conclude that the light seen has come into existence only with the throwing of a switch. Thus, when we observe movement, or "speed," we really are only considering the action of the vessel that reveals the light, and not the light itself.

The Kabbalist views the light itself, and the various vessels that contain and reveal it. The vessels, or capsules, exist on many levels and as we set further into subatomic areas, we will reach levels in which such capsules act well in excess of the scientist's view of the speed of light. Once that fallacious "speed of light" has been exceeded, two-way time travel—into the past or into the future—would occur. Thus, the universal Judaic hymn, "Adon O. Lam," says "and He was, and He is, and He will be," all at the same time. "He," of course, refers to the all-inclusive positive energy and Light of Wisdom that is God, and means that the essence of light is universal, with its presence found simultaneously and instantaneously, exclusive of the aspect of "time."

Einstein, for all his brilliance, failed to come to grips with many contradictions, steadfastly clinging to his "speed of light" theory, but everything points to the fact that on another level, there is no such things as a light speed barrier.

Knowledge is not measured as physical energy, as Einstein's theory of relativity attempts to do. When we speak of knowledge, we speak of consciousness itself, abstract a term as that may seem to be. Consciousness is simply a physical cable by which energy is transferred, and it is not limited to the speed of light. It is to light speed what the atomic world of Einstein is to the subatomic world of the future where different frames of reference, different rules, different laws and different principles must be used. From Newton to Einstein, we have come to the world of crystals, then to molecules, then to atoms, but the progression does not stop there. From the atom, we have proceeded to subatomic particles and now find ourselves at the threshold of true reality, which is consciousness existing far beyond the pitiful 5 or 10 per cent possessed by the average individual. With revelation of each new level of reality, from the mechanical to the conscious, each level will behave according to precise laws and principles no more contradictory than Einsteinian physics are to Newtonian.

Those laws and principles have room for many phenomena deemed fantasy by most laymen and virtually all scientists: paranormal abilities, including ESP (Extra Sensory Perception), precognition and telekinesis, parallel universe, metaphysical DNA that applies, not to physical development, but the soul. All exist in one frame of reference or another, yet surprisingly enough, they are rejected out of hand by people who have no trouble whatsoever accepting the fact that an astronaut aboard a space capsule can circumnavigate the globe in an hour at speeds unattainable within the atmosphere simply because he does so in the altered frame of reference of space.

That simple example will lead us into an area in which different frames of reference, different universal tracks and, consequently, different laws and principles of logic will be found: The area of parallel worlds or universe.

The principles of DNA, metaphysically viewed as reincarnation of DNA levels of a previous lifetime to determine the physical DNA level as we know it in this lifetime, may be used to illustrate the point as it applies to the soul. That leap, however, takes us below the quantum level, to the sub-quantum world of hidden variables. It is the physical world that causes the phenomena we observe on this worldly level, but it is from the underlying spaceless, timeless realm that events of ordinary reality, as we see them, emerge. The growing convergence of data from different sources already suggests the plurality of levels, both on our own physical plane and at the sub-quantum level. We are beginning to probe deeper for these varied levels of intelligent life form, but traditional scientists are driven to distraction by the resulting concepts of plurality.

Only 40 years ago, this concept was considered absurd. Nobel Laureate Irwin Schrodinger decided that the only sane explanation of quantum mechanics was that "the mind is simply something we cannot conceive of as plural." The point that Dr. Schrodinger overlooked was that the mind still exists within the physical realm. At that level, the mind cannot physically express more than one level at a time. It is in the sub-quantum area—in Kabbalistic terminology, the soul—that we find differing but parallel interrelated worlds and universes, each composed of endless universe tracks also called soul tracks. They are ultimately expressed as different patterns and outcomes for the same person depending upon the particular level of soul that emerges at any given time.

Different levels, layers and parallel tracks do not necessarily indicate different realities. How many of us behave in a certain way on Monday, then in another on Tuesday? Are we physically two different people? Certainly not. All the divergent entities are part of the one reality which is the all-embracing unity. Everything depends upon the particular soul track upon which the individual finds himself a passenger at any given time, and different tracks travelled will produce different results.

An important aspect of parallel tracks is the all-embracing seed. Of necessity, the seed must contain all the ultimate physical expression, from root to the ultimate and final destination, which is the fruit. At the seed level, the varied potential tracks all exist as one unified central force, part of the all-embracing unity concept. Why this fundamental picture of reality escapes the wisdom of the scientist is more of a mystery than the reality of people themselves. The parallel tracks that exist in our universe, depending upon which of them is taken, will determine the ultimate outcome for the individual.

We have already established through the Zohar that there are different layers that interact within the human body. So too are there different layers in the universe that act and react upon other layers. Results and outcomes depend upon which particular state is being used — a concept that can be expanded and used in consideration of the soul. Taking this aspect of parallel levels and universes, Isaac Luria stretches the point in "Gates of Reincarnation,"[16] declaring that within each individual soul on three different levels: soul, spirit and crude spirit. There are metaphysical transfers between levels, or wave lengths, which are channels in which a transfer of energy takes place.

When we speak of a transfer of energy, however, we are not referring to the energy itself, but rather to the revealment of that energy which comes through a vessel. When activated energy is revealed, we see what we think are streams of energy, but we really are observing the all pervading energy that suddenly is revealed to us by activity taking place in the channel. Thus, when we speak of "speed," we are speaking in terms of channels and vessels that reveal the essence of the light to which we refer. The ultimate is a certain level where one would not be dealing with light speed simply because there is no speed of light to discuss. That concept completely negates the principle of Einstein's theory of the speed of light and it also would obviate his fear that surpassing the speed of light would produce so many paradoxes. Yet, within the matrix exists the possibility of time travel. Since Einstein could not understand the paradoxes that seem to arise, he ruled out the possibility that there could be universes where light speed no longer exists, but we are gradually approaching just such an area. It is an area in which space-time no longer would take place and where past, present and future exist simultaneously.

In Kabbalistic terms, light is prevalent and all pervading. There is no space in this or any other universe that is empty of light, just as, at our level, there is no space empty of atoms. The parallel is, simply, that there are two kinds of atomic structures — the mass in which they have joined to become molecules of apparently solid matter and in an unjoined state through which one's head might pass with no sensation whatsoever. There may be more atoms in a cubic inch of air than in a cubic inch of tables, but in the air, they are unrevealed. As the table, in the case of atoms, is the vessel that reveals them, light does not become revealed without a vessel which gives rise to a wonderful paradox: Nothing can become revealed unless it first is concealed. At the human social level, a person dares not reveal himself in public unless he first is concealed in clothing.

When one delves into the inner essence of things, however, many layers of revealment will be encountered. Among other states of vessels, there is the vessel of the table, measured in time and space. Then there is the vessel of the atom, invisible to the naked eye, but revealed under a microscope. As we probe deeper and deeper, we will find other states revealed—states we consider consciousness. The table used in a previous example is a state of consciousness. Scientists today have developed a theory matching something long known in Kabbalah: The desire to receive, the vessel, is an intelligence. There is a state of consciousness called "table," another called "rock" and still another called "tree." And there is a state of consciousness called "man." All are different, yet all are conscious.[17]

Eugene Wigner, a Nobel prize-winning physicist, wrote of the unreasonable effectiveness of mathematics in the natural sciences in an essay titles "Two Kinds of Reality".[18] The first, he said, is "my own consciousness and the second, everyting else." Scientific knowledge leans on, and is impossible without, the type of knowledge we acquired in babyhood. Scientific knowledge is an infinitesmal fraction of the natural knowledge. "One might say," wrote Heisenberg, "that the human ability to understand may be, in a certain sense, unlimited. But the existing scientific concepts cover always only a very limited part of reality and the other part that has not yet been understood is infinite. Whenever we proceed from the known into the unknown, we may hope to understand, but we may have to learn at the same time a new meaning for the word understanding." The understanding is recognized even before it is rationally understood in detail."[19]

When Rabbi Ashlag referred in 1919 to positive, negative and central column concepts as "desires," it scarcely was appreciated how stunningly remarkable his view of reality was. Little did the world of physics then realize how this theory of intelligence, or consciousness of all matter, would bring us closer to the secret of our universe. Everything was, and is, thought. In "The Mysterious Universe," famed astrophysicist, Sir James Jean, wrote "The universe can be best pictured, although still very imperfectly and inadequately, as consisting of pure thought, the thought of what, for want of a wider word, we must describe as a mathematical thinker."

Rabbi Ashlag summed up thought in a word: "Desire." He said the power of mind and thought move through innumerable channels consisting mainly of a desire to receive, share and restrict.[20] This, perhaps, is what Niels Bohr, Einstein's greatest opponent in the quantum theory debate and recipient of a Nobel Prize in physics in 1922, a year after Einstein became a laureate, meant when he told his own son, "You are not thinking; you are merely logical."

Bohr did not recognize the profundity of his own statement. He was, in fact, stating that when one is connected to the inner space of thought, he is transcending the 5 per cent limiting realm of logic and reaching the understanding that exists long before it is rationally understood. According to Rabbi Ashlag, this is achievement of "Devekut," or communion with the original thought and its thought process.

From a Kabbalistic viewpoint, we have the language to discuss different states of consciousness, different levels, different kinds of vessels, different kinds of desires to receive, different kinds of intelligence and different levels of consciousness. There is only one kind of energy from a Kabbalistic viewpoint: The light of Wisdom. It is the same, no matter where it appears. The only thing that affects it is the nature of the vessel, or kind of consciousness, that receives it. Some kinds of consciousness reveal more light, others less. Different states of consciousness, different levels, different desires to receive all affect how much or how little light one perceives.

Ten years ago, the telephone system consisted of heavy cables that would send only a few messages at one time. A microchip now accomplishes the same task at far higher volume. The amount of electricity that enters any given home is the same. The difference is in the vessel, be it a power-devouring air conditioner, a 15-watt bulb or a 200-watt bulb. Such vessels, having different consciousnesses, determine the amount of energy they will reveal by means of their own concealment.

To sum up the meaning of technological advance, it is the removal of the physicality of a vessel, gradually drawing closer to the point at which, in apparent paradox, it would appear that the less the physical material, the more potent the energy flow; that as the vessel becomes smaller, the amount of energy passing through it increases.

As technology gradually approaches different levels of receiving and varying states of consciousness, it approaches, for all practical purposes, the speed of light and beyond. The tiny microchip now moves more messages at a far quicker pace than did its clumsy predecessor, the cable. It has less material, but the level of consciousness is far greater, not only in volume and density, but in speed as well. Computers move enormous amounts of information at a time, and as the vessel becomes smaller, it leads us inexorably toward the day when we will use hairline channels, then living channels constructed of proteins, and when the channels themselves become living organisms, the speed of light will be surpassed.

The transition is coming more swiftly than any scientist currently imagines. It will present a universe in which we will become accustomed to matter as energy itself. Then only will science realize that we are not speaking of the speed of light, but about the speed of vessels.

When a person attains an altered state of consciousness, he can be very material, but his physicality will begin to fade as he reaches toward a microchip state of consciousness. Thus has the computer put man into the back seat where his power lies in less, not more, materiality. Much today is written about the use of computers to foil the computers of an enemy and to jam his radar by sending counter signals on the same frequency, but the same does not stop there. Ultimately, the enemy radar sets a bit "smarter," with its computers programmed to jump from frequency to frequency and thus avoid the interference. Our equipment then can be programmed to track the shifting signals and automatically adjust to jam them again in an endless, expensive and counterproductive cycle. Computer systems locked in such a contest become dangerously obsolete in moments, yet billions of dollars will be spent on such systems simply to build our belief that we are not vulnerable. The futility of such an approach is painfully obvious, but the business of jumping from frequency to frequency is nothing new. Kabbalistic meditation does the same thing with frequencies that exist as parallel levels of the universe. Kabbalistic meditation, however, is designed to reveal the pervading internal Light of Wisdom, the only energy force which is all-pervading as the opposite of the force that is the Desire to Receive.

2

Desire: A Key to the Cosmos

Enough of science and of art;
Close up these barren leaves.
Come forth, and bring with you a heart
That watches and receives.

— William Wadsworth, *The Tables Turned*

THE DESIRE TO RECEIVE IS CENTRAL TO EVERYTHING IN COSMOS. No entity, from a stone to a human being, can exist without it, but it comes in many layers. The more sophisticated purify its denser attributes and the less corporeal it becomes, the more capable it is of transferring or communicating with energy. Remember, there is no such thing as an actual transfer of observed energy.

Wherever speed of light or transfer of energy occurs, vessels are merely revealing the apparent movement of the Light of Wisdom which is all pervading and does not change. In the intelligence of the desire to receive, we profess a system which, according to Grollier, is "A group of interacting, interrelating or interdependant elements forming, or regarded as forming, a collective entity." Systems usually include the transfer agent and the energy that is being transferred.

From the Kabbalistic viewpoint, there is a transfer of energy through a series of entities called different parts of the cable. When a system is devised, it stretches the concept of desire to receive, extending it just as the cable does. Each time a part of that system is activated, there is not, as commonly is accepted in physics, a transfer of energy, but rather a revealing of the energy that already is there. There is no transfer of energy, but there appears to be.

When I refer to a system, I specifically refer to the vessels that reveal the all-pervading energy that always has existed in an unrevealed state, such as atoms in the universe. Reference to systems, then different systems, more effective systems, then computer-jamming systems is a reference to different levels of vessels taking the desire to receive deeper and deeper to the point at which they touch the root. This is the difference in intelligence. What makes up the difference in intelligence at that point which is unseen? What causes differences at that point and what makes the differences between one system and another?

Intelligence has been defined as different desires to receive, but that is not the root of the matter. To arrive at the root where it all begins, one must get into subatomics where different levels of vessels, now unseen, consist of different gradations of the desire to receive, which is the root of intelligence. What makes the difference between one intelligence that is revealing the all-pervading energy force and another? Where the desire to receive has been transmuted to a desire to impart, and depending upon the degree to which the desire to receive has been transmuted, the grade of revealment of the Light of Wisdom will be determined. Different, or altered, states of consciousness, are different levels of spirituality, and the altering of the desire to receive for oneself to one of imparting is the same thing.

The purer the internal energy of the vessel is, the greater is its intelligence. The revealment in this system is copious because an entire system, with an infinite number of segments, is involved. When we activate the infinite number of entities which comprise the system, the speed of which has appeared to scientists as the speed of light, only the purest desire to receive is brought into play.

As Rabbi Shimon Bar Yohai put it, for us to understand the inner machinations and workings of the metaphysical area, which, for all practical purposes, remains concealed, we must resort to finding its manifest state on a physical level. Finding what we consider to be the branch of the root, we will be able to pinpoint the metaphysical aspect of the subject under discussion, which is different gradations of the desire to receive. An article by Owen Davies in the November 1982 issue of Omni magazine provided an example of the method by which different gradations and levels of purity may be established.

Davies wrote of electrophoresis, a sophisticated chemical process used to purify drugs and other complex compounds: "On earth, gravity tends to remix the desired product with the impurities, even as the equipment is trying to separate them. Electrophoresis can still produce very pure drugs, but only in small quantities. The larger the machine on earth, and the more material you put into it, the less efficient is the process, and the more contaminated is the product that comes out. So MacDonald Douglas Research decided to do away with gravity, packed the separations into a narrow box six feet long, and locked it on the wall of the space shuttle's cabin. We knew the machine had worked properly almost as soon as we got it back. The purification was just as effective as it was on earth, but we were able to put 400 times as much material through the machine."

Gravity, from a Kabbalistic view, is the interiority of the desire to receive. As you go "up the ladder" and move out in the magnetic field of gravity, you experience another kind of field wherein gravity ceases to exist. There, the coarseness, the density, of the impurities, which desires to receive inevitably contain, also cease to exist. Where gravity declines, purity rises in degree.

Getting back to the innermost energy factor that exists in systems or in vessels, channels or cables, where the greatest desire to receive exists, so does the greatest lack of speed, but the least desire to receive is not the most pure.

Purity is the ability to transmute the intense desire to receive for oneself alone to one of imparting that which is received. Friction prevents speed and revealment of the Light of Wisdom. The system is not pure. The purer the system becomes in dealing with proteins and other living organisms, the more gradations there will be to the point of infinity.

The ultimate intelligence would be the endless world, where the desire to receive is as pure as the desire to impart. That never will be achieved at our level of life on earth. We would need to go beyond the aspect of time established by Einstein as 186,000 miles per second and the proposition that we cannot achieve that is a complete fallacy which should be done away with as quickly as possible. It does not serve us correctly on our level, let alone upon levels sought through different states of consciousness where time and space no longer are factors. Quantum and relativity theories theoretically have established that there is no aspect of space/time, but only when we at last understand that intelligence/consciousness is in a very pure state can we experience a lessening of the space/time influence.

Altered states of consciousness, from a Kabbalistic view, occur when an individual achieves different levels of desires to receive, which are different levels of consciousness.

When television networks broadcast on their own frequencies (which are their own peculiar systems of the overall desire to receive), we are inclined to accept the notion that the information being transmitted from the broadcasting station originates there. From a Kabbalistic point of view, however, the information always has existed, but in potential form merely awaiting the channel or revealing instrument that ultimately will make it manifest. Information is an integral part of the all pervading Light of Wisdom, which includes all information that was, is and will be. Channels, cables and systems all are part of the intelligence, or desire to receive, which itself is the vessel that reveals the information that already exists. Higher or lower frequencies and jamming all are different variations of the revealing system. Only here, on earth, can we experience "change," otherwise known as the advance of technology. Information, therefore, is only energy that needs to be revealed.

To have the power of precognition, teleportation or transfer of energy from one person to another means only to stretch one's system. How far it will stretch and where it can be directed depends upon the individual system. If one has a total frequency that can pervade the earth, he will instantly reveal energy that exists throughout the world. The longer the frequency, in terms of revealment and distance, the more power it possesses. The "Voice of America" pervades the earth because its creators devised a desire to receive system designed for such widespread play. Information and energy are the same thing in that system, just as they are in all systems.

ESP is nothing more than a connection made with another person. It is no more mysterious than a telephone call, though prior to the invention of that instrument, the concept of a telephone was most mysterious indeed. To practice ESP, one must engulf the person he is trying to contact into his own system, but this is possible only by means of a pure desire to receive in its pure, unadulterated state in which balance of genuine desire to impart is included. The process, however, also poses a dark side addressed in the Bible[21] by the concept of Armageddon. In the Armageddon to come, the Russians, who have attached a high priority to research into the matter, conceptually could engulf us, instantly tapping any information at hand from those who, having neither knowledge of nor belief in such forces, will have no defense against it. The connection is made via that frequency which instantaneously reveals meaning closest to the Light of Wisdom and its desire to share, but desire to receive is a powerful force in its own right, and even without purity it can be made to serve evil purposes.

When desire is pure, an affinity, a similarity, is established with the Light of Wisdom and the similarity completes the connection. The closer one is to the Light, the closer he is to the desire to share, and hence, to intelligence. Closeness, in this case, has no reference to distance. When people are close to one another, it is because they share similar intelligences and desires to receive. So great is the power at this level that pure energies come into play, energies that are not in contest with things at the corporeal level. But how does one achieve such an altered state of consciousness? Rabbi Shimon Bar Yohai had the answer. "Look around," he said, "because that is where you are going to find your answer."

Look around and find, for example, a walnut. It has what we call a

Klippa, or shell. Remove that shell and you have the internal aspect of the walnut. All physical things have shells—even people. How often have you heard someone, in exasperation, say, "You cannot reach that man." What does that mean? On a physical level, he certainly can be reached. He can be touched, pushed, smitten or caressed, but move one step up the ladder to the metaphysical level and you will detect the magnetic field he has built around himself to keep others out. It is his Klippa, his shell.

Shells can be very thick indeed. They present us from setting deep into the interior of whatever they surround and at both physical and metaphysical levels, such shells are constructed of the desire to receive, which is the exact opposite of the inner consciousness, which is the desire to share. The two are not on similar frequencies. They are on frequencies far apart and, as a result, there is less revealment of the energy involved. The only way in which an ESP connection can be made is if one can connect with himself, eliminating much of his own desire to receive and thus growing spiritually. Spiritual growth means nothing more than getting closer to the ultimate vessel which reveals the Light. When we speak of a person who manages to achieve greater alternate states of consciousness, we really are discussing one capable of connecting to the frequency or channel of an increasingly pure vessel and the purer the vessel, the greater the amount of the Light of Wisdom it will reveal. The degree to which this energy is tapped will depend upon the degree to which physicality is diminished.

It is not easy to achieve that diminution. It requires conscious effort on the part of the sojourner who first must rid himself of his inborn desire to receive for the self alone. This is accomplished through prayer and meditation which may be launched by the beginner as a program of halting all extraneous thought for 10 minutes a day as he seeks the multitude of levels of frequencies by which his desire may be accomplished. To halt thought, however—to turn off the constant internal dialogue which all of us carry on constantly with ourselves—is the equivalent of halting a runaway team of horses. It can be done, but only with deep dedication and long practice. This is not the place in which to delve into Kabbalistic meditation, a subject fit for another volume. Suffice to say that one must conquer physicality before one can achieve the altered state of consciousness necessary to move beyond it.

The difference between a computer main frame and its microchips is physicality. The less the physicality — and as microchips dwindle toward the molecular level, computers become increasingly powerful — the greater the similarity is to that internal energy which does not move and has no speed of its own but exists rather as pure frequency. It may appear to the observer at the physical level that movement takes place, but the energy is there in total pervasiveness all the time, transcending the concept of lightspeed.

With those points established, we now can begin to understand the meaning of Creation in the Bible. We are told, in Genesis,[22] about people who lived at the time of Adam and for several generations thereafter who enjoyed extraordinarily long lifetimes. Adam lived 930 years and Methusela held the record at 976. Mankind's life expectancy subsequently declined to an average span of 40 years and, in the past century, gradually has begun to rise again, but the Bible addresses neither phenomenon because the Bible generally is not concerned with recorded history. Genesis, rather, reveals coded phenomena designed to explain parallel universe, metaphysics and other frames of reference, including the Age of Aquarius in which we now live and in which technological advances of the past 30 years far exceed any that have taken place in millenia of the past.

Many things called unknown or unknowable by modern man are revealed in the Bible, but we shall deal here only with a few by explanation of the all-pervading energy of intelligence which offers itself to all of us for beneficial connection. One problem, for example, that has baffled mankind in general and scientists in particular for years is the sudden extinction, after what scientists tell us was 150 million years of rule, of the dinosaurs. The list of suspected reasons for their demise is as long as human ingenuity can make it, but all the theories have one thing in common and that is catastrophe.

While the harebrained ideas of such mavericks as Emanuel Velakovsky ("Worlds in Collision") have shown the importance of catastrophe as a means of evolutionary change, none really has achieved scientific acceptance. That is because the aim of science is to discover only those natural laws which function with the precision of order. If such were the sole stock of the Creator, the principles of evolution would be rigid with regularity. In the scientific view, some unsettling, freakish extraterrestrial event that put an end to millions and millions of years of orderly evolution just doesn't seem to be the proper answer, and in this case, the scientists are right.

The truth is, the dinosaurs never were and are not now extinct. We have lived among them for centuries, simultaneously blessing them for their favors and regarding them with primordial fear. We call them reptiles.

The Bible tells us that before the fall of Adam, "There were giants in the earth in those days,"[23] and indeed there were. Coding of Genesis tells us that Adam himself may have towered 100 feet tall[24] in the metaphysical paradise of Eden where, until the desire to receive for themselves alone overcame them, Adam and Eve reigned in complete obedience to the laws of nature and the universe. With the fall, however, their world dwindled, diminishing both in stature and in the Light of Wisdom, until Adam was but a weary farmer of our accustomed physical proportion tilling the soil in a field where the once great dinosaurs now skittered as innocuous lizards and snakes. You may not find *Tyrannosaurus rex* in the meadow, but you will find the pathetic remnant of his progeny, not extinct, but utterly unrecognized. If that flies in the face of Darwin's evolutionary explanations, so be it, but it also would explain to fundamentalists why no "thunder lizards" trod the gang plank of Noah's Ark.

The foregoing may strike the average citizen, locked as he is in his linear world of time, space and motion, as the image of a febrile mind, but in Kabbalah, there are many different universes, different veils, different cosmic influences that structure different kinds of life, both on a metaphysical and on a physical plane. We are told by the Zohar,[25] and by "Gates of Reincarnation,"[26] that every man contains multiple levels of parallel universe,. and only in this context can the code of Genesis be understood. The lower level of man's multiplicity is called crude spirit. Above that lies another sphere called spirit and the upper level is called soul. Within this context, Kabbalah introduces a new way of thinking about old concepts. For example, within the levels of parallel universes lie parallel states of consciousness which lead mankind back to various levels of the desire to receive, which, in itself, is a consciousness. It too, however, is further divided into infinite levels.

This path will lead us to the answer regarding a paradox discussed earlier: Time travel and the speed of light. When we approach the speed of light in the Einsteinian sense, space and time cease to exist. At that point, time travel, at the level of consciousness where time ceases to be, can begin. It is the phase at which the level of gravitation also vanishes in a gravitational field that effectively prohibits acceleration of space and time. In the parallel universes of the metaphysical, time travel begins above crude spirit, pure spirit reigns. Upon reaching the level of spirit, the individual enters into a new level of consciousness, or an altered state of consciousness, that consists of pure awareness, which alters the level of desire to receive, bringing it into harmony with the Light of Wisdom which has only one characteristic: the desire to share and that is not governed by space/time which can exist only at the level of limitation. As established, within the Light of Wisdom nothing is lacking, and when we reach it, finally bereft of the desire to receive for ourselve alone, we have made the outer space connection.

Once that connection is made, through prayer, meditation and a conscious determination to restrict the desire to receive, which is, by the way, our sole possible exercise of "free will," past events literally can be witnesses either as flashes from previous incarnations or through dreams which can illuminate the future as well as the past. Such revelations lie in the spiritual realm of Ruach in which there is no manifestation of time, space or motion as we perceive them in Nefesh, the crude spirit realm in which most of us dwell. Nefesh alone allows the body to age and deteriorate. In Nefesh alone can there be lies, deceit and death, along with that sense of mortality that limits human vision to the here and now. The soul that can rise to the parallel universe of Ruach, where Adam lived before the fall, is affected by nothing in Nefesh, which explains why the so-called "Grandfather Paradox" is no paradox at all. Any adventurer going back in time to prevent the marriage of his grandparents would have to do so in the realm of Ruach, and the physical union of his grandparents never existed there.

The key to time travel at the level of Ruach is the ability to share. Nothing else will put the soul in close proximity with the Light of Wisdom, but once enveloped in that all pervasive, motionless, light perceptions of time and space fade like dreams and all the time traveler must do to witness the signing of the Magna Carta or see Moses receiving the Ten Commandments is decide that he is at Runnymeade or on Mount Sinai. Under such travel arrangements, I may say that I saw you at a given time on a certain street corner and you may protest that you were not there. Further inquiry, however, may reveal that even for a fleeting moment you thought of the location or planned to go there in the future, and that is the moment at which I saw you. Time travel literally is at the fingertips of anyone who is willing to let himself be free of desire to receive for himself alone and, by that means, find the true desire to share all that he can obtain from the Light of Wisdom.

Before the sin of Adam, which was a negation of the Light of Wisdom, the entire world existed at the level of Ruach, unfettered by the chains of space and time, unshadowed by entropy and death. When Adam "fell," he literally fell from that blessed state of consciousness into Nefesh, dragging the world down with him. His descendants have been struggling to regain the Eden of his creation ever since. They have failed simply because they never have realized one central truth: Most of the tragedies that befall us do so because we have willed them to, blindly and carelessly, by the power of words. God created cosmos with a word, and that power, diluted many times by our own egocentric desire to receive with little thought of imparting, was passed to His creatures. We learn from the Zohar that one must be very careful in the manner by which he addresses catastrophe, illness or other life-threatening situations. To speculate verbally as to what might happen activates another state of consciousness that almost inevitably creates the occurrence being so fearfully discussed. The thought becomes the reality; the word becomes the deed. There are many such states of consciousnees and not all of them are benign, but because man never can separate himself from the universe, all of them, even the lowest, contain power with which only fools will trifle. The soul's only defense as it journeys through the myriad levels that make up the metaphysical universe is to achieve at-one-ment (remove the hyphens and receive yet another word of power) with the Light of Wisdom, and one of the best road maps clarifying the way to that goal is Kabbalistic astrology as explained by the Book of Splendor, when it says, "As the body of man is divided and subdivided into sections and all are poised upon levels of different magnetic fields and intelligence, by which each react and interact with the other, although remaining independent, so is the entire world based upon parallel and different levels by which each section, each segment of the universe is related and interrelated with each other. And upon man rests the entire movement and strings of the universe.[27]

Two incredible statements: Man is the determining director of movement in this universe and man is structured as a carbon copy of everything in that universe! Science probes for the answers that religion takes on faith, and astrology is the bridge between them.

To date, for all his technological advances, the only place where men have walked beyond the earth is its moon. Astrology permits one to go farther and acquire knowledge about all the other planets in the solar system and determine the extent of their astral influences. The pure scientist may shake his head in despair at such a statement, but once again, Zohar I makes it clear: "The body of man is related to our entire galaxy and universe." In depth analysis of the body, along with understanding which planet or which part of our galaxy relates to each different section of man, the different parts of man will open new vistas to the heavens. We then, in turn, by proper analysis and investigation from a Kabbalistic point of view, can probe and penetrate inner depths, the internal energy forces of different parts of the body. The Kabbalist, then, is in a position to understand the internal energy force and intelligence of the planets."

In this age of quantum mechanics and microchips, the education of an individual cannot possibly be complete without some knowledge of the basic fundamentals of science and their historical background.

What the Zohar presents in light of the theory of relativity opens to the scientist of tomorrow as well as the layman a new understanding of the laws of nature and of the theory of relativity itself. The theory of relativity touches many aspects of the physical world. It stretches from the atomic realm to the make-up of the universe. The Zohar repeatedly states, "That which is below is above and that which is above is below."[28] Reinforced with the theory of relativity, everything really is connected and interdependently related. The revelation of the Zohar, with careful scrutiny of the anatomy of the individual, allows us to learn exactly what exists in the realm of the galaxy and in the realm of undiscovered celestial objects as well.

It therefore comes as no surprise that the famed Italian Kabbalist, Shabbatai Donolo also was a physician. His famous work on the Kabbalah, referred to as the *Book of Wisdom*, explains in precise detail the composites and relativities of one planet to another. Donolo's Book of Remedies contains a great deal of material drawn from his knowledge of astrology which undoubtedly was based upon his comprehension of the Kabbalah.

The *Book of Wisdom* provides a mass of information on the study of astrology. Without it, astrology would remain incomprehensible. Without this thorough insight into the essential and fundamental structures and composites of our great galaxy, the study would remain dichotomous, with astrology not relating to scientific ideas as to what constitutes the universe. Donolo's information paves the way for the study of astrology finally to become a respected science.

The origins of astrology, and hence of astronomy, are lost in the mists of time. When man first attempted to arrange the structure of his life, his attention naturally was drawn to the heavens which seemed to hold the key to structural order. The regular cycle of day and night and the steady rhythm of the seasons were reason enough to look skyward. What was lost, though it has existed since the time of Abraham's Book of Formation, were the formulae that explained it all.

As a result of that loss, star worship came into being. One who delved into the science and study of astrology was considered an idol worshipper which, from a Kabbalistic viewpoint, is far from the truth. When man accepted the sun, stars and planets as deities to be worshipped for the benefits they might bestow, they worshipped for a specific reason: They wanted to make use of celestial bodies for personal gain. The physical beneficence of the celestial bodies alone was considered. No one really attempted to make an in-depth study of the internal, or spiritual, structure and in that narrow view, the truth was lost.

Early civilizations considered the celestial deities to be their rulers. They accepted the proposition that astral influences existed, but they could do little to overcome them. Thus did misinformation begin to creep in. If astral influences are negative, from a Kabbalistic point of view, how to jam or deflect them becomes of paramount importance, and prayer swiftly became the vehicle by which the supplicant hoped to achieve that power. The Hebrew word for prayer, however, is tafel, which literally means secondary, a reflection, the periphery. Prayer is not central to the issue. Prayers are merely channels and, like a driverless vehicle or a telephone line with no speaker to use it, prayers become a nullity. The business of prayer remains big business in the modern world of religion, but like its idolatrous root, which turned such stars as Beutelgeuse or Altair into gods and put a deity named Apollo into the cockpit of the sun, prayer is a myth.

Prayer, from a Kabbalistic point of view, is merely a tapping of energy, just as the aforementioned stars are bottled-up energies in a metaphysical cosmos. Prayer is not an appeal to a higher court; a plea for mercy, justice or gain. The Kabbalist knows the channels that convey the only power worth having—the one that neutralizes the desire to receive for the self alone. This is the crippler that renders what the religious call prayer little more than empty rhetoric. Pity the man who anchors the destiny of his soul in the shifting, treacherous sands of what men call prayer.

Prayer is a powerful thing, but few, unhappily, know how to wield it. Even as we engage in prayer, most of us wander far afield, planning schedules for the next day, worrying about business or simply day dreaming. As a body of people, we prayed fervently during the holocaust, but that did not save 6 million Jews from the crematoria. Many prayed while a similar holocaust annihilated the nation of

Cambodia, but prayer apparently rescued few of Pol Pot's victims. It is all a question of proper channels. If I want to watch the 11 o'clock news and I tune in at 9, I will not receive the program sought no matter how fervently I desire it. If I insist on watching Channel 2, all the power of technology will not permit me to see programming on Channel 4. Every two hours, our prayers are influenced by a different planet. To pray effectively, we must know, be connected and understand. Otherwise, our efforts are worth little more than idol (idle) worship.

To overcome the old, false gods, who, like the human souls that invented them, seem to reincarnate through the ages in one form or another, one must use any number of the keys offered by Kabbalah, and one of the most effective keys on the ring is astrology, once its internal, spiritual, structure is revealed. Astrology is both a science and an art, but the mechanics of its science as well as the techniques of its art are bound to the understanding and interpretation of the internal cosmic influence that heavenly bodies have on the individual. We must, therefore, know about the scientific basis of astronomy to understand why the universe is structured as it is. We must achieve a thorough understanding of *why* celestial bodies behave the way they behave, and the relation of the way they behave to the position in which they find themselves at any given time. Then, and then only, can we hope to bridge the astrology/astronomy gap and at least consider them one science, not two. This is important because observable behaviorial patterns are merely manifestations of their celestial bodies. What is most important is to seek new answers to Kabbalah's most important question: Why?

The answer lies in a metaphysical concept that the seed becomes the tree, thus revealing that which is revealed first must be concealed. The primary cause, however, remains after manifestation, as does the seed: Once planted, forever concealed.

How often have you done or said something totally unplanned and unexpected and wondered, often ruefully, why you did it? You may winnow your mind without finding the seed of the action. It did its work, but it remains hidden. Yet the key to understanding no longer is hidden. Kabbalalistic astrology, backed by the Sefer Yetsirah, the earliest known work of Judaic mysticism, can be a road map to motives. The Sefer Yetsirah is remarkable in that it provides most of the answers that are necessary to establish astrology as a science.

The enormous growth and popularity astrology has enjoyed in the last 20 years probably is related to the Age of Aquarius. The fact that astrology, in the latter half of the 20th century became acceptable, even respectable, can be traced to Aquarian influence. Nor is it by chance that knowledge of Kabbalah, at the same time, has become widespread and available to the layman. Ancient secrets now are in the domain of all, and no longer is it necessary to accrue vast amounts of knowledge before delving into them.

Through the scientific structure provided by the Sefer Yetsirah and the many commentaries written upon it, it is my hope that a proper understanding of the system may be rendered, and while I do not deny that one can achieve much knowledge and help through the conventional path of astrology, I must stress the dichotomy between science and astrology. They cannot be completely bridged unless and until there is in-depth understanding of astronomy and the universe with all its physical bodies. Kabbalah takes this one giant step forward, allowing a greater number of "whys" still facing and perplexing the scientific community to be answered.

Serious changes in recent years seem to hold great promise for the progress of astrology. They inevitably will change attitudes toward its serious study. The use of natural explanations are working to relate astrology to the scientific community, and this book will identify a great deal of common ground between the two. Noting the Zohar, rhythms and cycles of the universe have a deep impact upon the rhythms and cycles of biology and anatomy. A sincere and successful partnership between astrology and science is likely to result through dissemination of this information.

Unhappily, at the moment, astrology and Kabbalah share one unfortunate attribute in the public mind. Neither is believed. Kabbalah is scorned on principle by many who never have heard the word, as it is by those who have heard nothing but the word. Reactions range from fear to humanistic pragmatism, but lack of belief predominates, all of which is sheer folly because to use the word "believe" is to admit that one does not know. Thus, attititudes taken toward astrology in many quarters, despite its recent popularization, are based not upon what it is, but upon what is not known. The Zohar I am about to quote will rankle many astrologers and true believers, even though I do not necessarily find contradiction between the Zohar and conventional astrology: "And the wisdom of their wisdom was lost." The Zohar states[29] that "was lost" refers to the wisdom of the ancient Egyptians whose internal understanding forever has been concealed, even though the Egyptians in the day of their power did not know it. The Zohar goes on to explain: "for they do not know in the initial creation of celestial bodies, but only in their manifested uses. Their knowledge is based on the changes that are observed in the world we experience, in their travel, and in the way they are made use of."

Thus, from the Zohar, do we arrive at the correct conclusion that the ancient Egyptians' philosophy of astrology was not based on the internal structure of creation, meaning the original "Why?" Knowledge is the mother of creation as well as of invention and that is where the action really exists. This, no less than the seed or the sperm that is the cause of the ultimate effect.

The Zohar's explanation of the foregoing verse merely follows the general pattern of duality upon which all creation is constructed: The physical and the metaphysical, the external and the internal. Man, in whom we perceive both a body and a soul, is no differently structured. Thus, it is easy to understand that the only way in which we can control another individual is not by the external means of physical restraint, but through the internal control of his mind. Those who pursued "hearts and minds" during the Vietnam war were on the right track, but ultimately, they failed, and all the physical military might of the United States ultimately proved futile in America's first unwinnable war. The objective, therefore, of Kabbalistic astrology as it is approached in this book is to reveal both the internal and external composites of the entire universe, including man.

Once we have acquired this knowledge, we then will be on the threshold of a major breakthrough in interplanetary communication. According to the Kabbalah, all transfers of energy are, in effect, transfers of intelligence. To speak of extraterrestrial "intelligent life" is to speak of nothing more. No little green men or space ships roaring in warp drive out of "Star Trek" are necessary. Transfers of energy, however they are made throughout the universe, are transfers of information, and where there is a transfer of information, intelligence becomes a power and "mind power" no longer may be excluded from the realm of scientific inquiry.

Kabbalah has given us the names whereby we can pinpoint any particular exchange of energy, rendering interplanetary communication, with its transfer of energy/information, no more wondrous than a similar transfer made between individuals over a telephone. Much has been made in the past 20 years of signals that seem to be coming from interstellar space. Most have been traced to such enigmatic phenomena as quasars or pulsars with little credence in the scientific community, at least, for great civilizations as a source. From a Kabbalistic point of view, no such civilizations exist beyond the confines of the planet earth, but that does not mean that the signals first detected by such endeavors as Project Ozma are devoid of true, and useful, intelligence. Intelligence is simply the kind of energy that is manifested at one point and perceived at another at a given time. There is nothing random or unchoreographed about the dance of the electrons that comprise cosmos.

Nor is choreography missing in what the Soviet Union is doing to harness these forces. Investigate reporter Jack Anderson recently reported that the Soviet scientific establishment, unlike our own, has put a top priority on metaphysical studies with an eye toward controlling what potentially is a cosmic communications system utilizing extrasensory perception and all that it implies. Such powers, once understood and controlled, potentially could wreak devastation upon an enemy nation by driving its people toward madness, mass suicide and the collapse of vital institutions, a potential unhappily scorned by Western scientists who, in their zeal for intellectual "purity," lump all things metaphysical with ouija boards, tea leaves and things that go bump in the night. What they cannot squeeze into a test tube or scan with a mass spectrometer simply doesn't exist for them. It is an attitude that carries deadly implications.

The Kabbalist always has known how to tap the forces of

intelligence that pervade the universe. All of them have names, set forth as sephirot in the tree of life. They are channels that carry such concepts as judgement, mercy, wisdom and victory the way a cable carries electrical current, and make no mistake, they are very real. Every event, every action, every idea is connected through the human mind by the network that is cosmos. Space is mind and we are part of it, but Western science has no idea what or where mind is. Eastern science may learn to know, to our peril.

Let us examine the full range of such power. Humans always have controlled it, but in nearly all cases, without conscious intent. We remember with horror the holocaust of World War II, but do we remember the festering hatred that caused it? Every action of man is carried by the channels of cosmos whether man knows it or not. Every earthquake, every supernova, every war is the direct result of violence and hatred in the hearts of men. We have, at our fingertips, the ability to recreate Eden. Instead, we build nuclear warheads and prepare for unspeakable hell.

Every one of us participates in the process. Negative thinking triggers negative action, just as positive thinking triggers the positive. Unhappily, we seem to prefer to negative and, in a world as small as ours, the impact is massive. The slightest deception, the pettiest crime, the smallest injustice committed by the least of us is part and parcel of a world conspiracy of hatred that can and will, if it is not turned around, eventually destroy the world. Control of the negative was the means by which Egypt enslaved the world prior to Exodus. Can any of us take lightly the thought that, given such power and the conscious control of it, the Soviet Union would do less today? And it is the Soviet Union that is looking beyond the physical boundaries.

Here, then, is what Kabbalists have known for centuries, and what their scientists well might discover:

The one star, Shabat, deactivates the desire to receive on the metaphysical plane where, the Zohar tells us,[30] there are 70 stars, representing seven sephirot and offering 70 facets of evil and 70 of good. They do cosmic battle every Friday and, if the unconscious actions of man sway that battle, what might the conscious actions of those who might select evil as the means to their ends accomplish?

Answer that question and suddenly the mere physicality of a nuclear detonation becomes little more than a footnote in the tale of terror.

The reality of anything physical has changed considerably since the discovery of modern quantum theory. Originally, the physical universe and our thoughts about it were believed unrelated and separate. Quantum physics shows us that what we can visualize actually is what we can see. Our mental picture of the universe, and the way the universe appears to us, basically are one and the same. The world of thought is not isolated from the physical world but, on the contrary, is closely bound up in it. Through our five senses, the mind is the recipient of a constant flow of information and of intelligent life forms of energy. The mind either stimulates the manifestation of new thoughts or existings ones. What, however, is the mind? This intriguing question long has been the favorite topic of debate among philosphers and religionists, and today, science studies the question through psychoanalysis and brain research. Though much seems to be obvious, the mechanism whereby matter acts upon the mind, and, more importantly, that which triggers the mind and its mental activity into the physical expression of mind over matter remains one of the most elusive phenomena facing the scientific community. How far does mind power extend? What are its limitations? Where, precisely, is the power of the mind located?

Wherever the answers lie, one thing is certain: Intelligence, or mind power, does exist. The French genecist, Francois Jacob, once said that the reason physics became ruler of the pack was that physics was the first to have its own language. That language was mathematics, but then something happened. We discovered a world beyond the five senses and everything changed. The language of mathematics no longer was capable of addressing thought, metaphysics or the unseen, but still very real, world. The principle of uncertaintly prevails and there no longer is a language to explain it away. It becomes dizzying to think of mass and particles that exist, yet patently do not exist, and that forces any good theoretical physicist to let go of solid ground and learn to become a mystic. In this, the Kabbalistic view becomes the only logic. The entire intelligence system of the universe, with its multiplicity of signals, is the direct result of the actions of man and therefore provides a complete interface of man's behavior.

"Star Wars"[31] — be they the property of George Lucas or Ronald Reagan — are nothing new. "Star Wars," in their broadest sense, were common in Moses' day as a quote from Zohar II will indicate: "And Moses assembled the children of Israel separately and gave them the Sabbath a new, saying "Six days shall work be done. Do not kindle any fire throughout your domain upon the Sabbath day."[32] Herein lies the supreme mystery, revealed only to those versed in the Supreme Wisdom: On the sixth day, when nightfall is due to begin, a brilliant star appears in the north accompanied by seventy other stars. That star smites the others, absorbing them all into itself, so that one takes the place of all seventy. The same star becomes enlarged and becomes a fiery mass, blazing on all sides. The flaming mass then extends itself around a thousand mountains which ultimately become a mere thread. After this, the fiery mass draws out from within itself a variety of colors. The first is a green color and when the green color appears, the fiery mass raises itself and plunges into the midst of the green color, establishing its presence within the case of it. Then the fiery mass of the star attracts within its interior a white cosmic color force. It then ascends and again invades the inner cosmic energy force of that color, occupying its internal cosmic center. The same cosmic event occurs with all known colors, all of which it thrusts outside, focusing itself more intensely toward the middle until it approaches that hidden point where the energy center exists and derives its light therefrom."

This amazing and profound section of the Zohar not only provides a new dimension of the subatomic world, but it focuses upon the enormous influence and power of astral body intelligence as well. The real "Star Wars" is the battle of man that becomes manifest on a planetary level. The signals we seem to be receiving from other civilizations really are transfers of energy that have originated right here on earth and have become manifest at all levels. The higher the level, the lesser the material aspect and the more refined the energy itself is. Thus, as noted in the foregoing Zohar, earth time and man's behavior produce incredible energy reaction and interaction at the cosmic level. At that level, the refinement of the cosmic consciousness of purer vessels inevitably produce greater intensities of energy transfer and revealment.

It is important to remember that cosmic events, illustrated by the parable of the Zohar quoted, always have been and always will be under human control, albeit most of the time without conscious intent. The Nazi holocaust was not merely a random horror. It was the result of a building hatred that became a channel for mass murder. We have at our fingertips the means by which we could recreate an Eden on earth simply by benevolent mass action, but that never will happen until the mass of men understand that they, through the mass action of hatred and violence, are creating just the opposite. Nations go on building nuclear warheads and with them, a cataclysm that could end the human race, but in a world so small as ours, even the tiniest crime or negative thought helps fuel the race toward death while the level of pure awareness eludes us.

It does not elude the Kabbalist, nor must it remain beyond the reach of anyone. In an altered state of consciousness, time ceases to be a factor and the perceived lag between cause and effect vanishes with it. The Age of Aquarian influence will find our civilization preoccupied with rational science. Our entire civilization will be dominated by and based upon science and technology, but those disciplines ultimately must rest upon the humanity of Aquarius which is depicted by the symbol of this sign of the zodiac. Aquarius is a human figure shown in a kneeling position. His urn of cosmic water rests upon one shoulder and its contents flow out in front of him. The internal consciousness of the eleventh sign is simple. According to the Zohar[33] and the Sefer Yetzirah,[34] the inner recesses of cosmic Aquarian thought hold the elements of sharing, right column, humanity. Sharing consciousness is an understanding of the oneness of all mankind which, in turn, indicates that Aquarius represents the dissemination of knowledge and the sharing of thought energy telepathically through brain waves.[35] Thus, Aquarius has become associated with the space age in which communication through the media contains less of the physical corporeal material of that function in times past. The Aquarian is involved with people. "Love thy

Neighbor"[36] is his motto and there are no boundaries to be considered. Space is the limit for the power of water which is the sharing concept. The Aquarian age, therefore, is the true harbinger of knowledge, for in this eleventh sign, the desire to receive continues to diminish. It is precisely for this reason that the sign is closely associated with the coming of the age of the Messiah; the stripping away of the limitations of man, paving the road to universal freedom.

Our present high-tech society, therefore, has emerged as a direct result of the Aquarian Age. Cosmically, it is the symbol of high-speed communication via space-borne satellite and of the removal of dense corporeality that marked earlier heavy and cluttered systems. For the first time in history, we are experiencing a diminution of that internal intelligence called "desire to receive for oneself alone" and the result is seen not only in permutations of rational science but in unprecedented interest in spiritual teachings and the love movements of recent decades. From the "flower power" of the 1960s to the microchip of the 1980s, all may be attributed directly to the astral influence of the Age of Aquarius.

Science is not the cause of these changes, nor will science be the cause of ultimate human relationships which, hopefully, will result in a grand tearing down of barriers between man and his fellow man — barriers constructed of the desire to receive for oneself alone. Man, however, always will be the determining factor as to where this manifestation of the Aquarian Age will lead us. Will science and technology be harnessed for peaceful purposes, leading us to interdependency, interrelation and inseparateness, or will they fail the golden potential of the age because mankind fails the challenge of the age?

From a Kabbalistic point of view, all things now lead in one direction: Quantum, the objective of which is Love Thy Neighbor. When that is achieved by the mass of men, the entire universe, both the seen and the unseen, will be revealed as they presently exist as a single, unified whole. Our universe is perceived as fragmented only because mankind is fragmented.

The point recalls a long session I had in 1973 with Emanuel Velikovsky, a most imaginative and controversial astronomer and physicist. We spent many hours together at Princeton arguing the very points set forth here. The thrust he simply could not bear came when I opened the Zohar[37] and said, "Dr. Velikovsky, all technology, all of science and its direction, including the movement of the stars, including the war of stars, will be completely dependent upon the action of man and his relationship and interrelationship with that which is around him. If that relationship of humankind becomes manifested within a concept of 'Love Thy Neighbor,' then we can be assured the result of which will be science and technology meeting the needs and demands of our universe and providing peaceful, harmonious objectives rather than for the sake of science alone. If, on the other hand, man cannot learn to adjust, compromise and live with his fellow man, then we will be the determining factor for science and technology to lead us into chaos and ultimate total destruction. This ultimate, total destruction will be, as described in the Zohar, a horrible war of stars which all of us will witness and which will be a result of and the culmination of our actions."[38]

Velikowsky could not tolerate this concept. He could not accept the proposition that man is not just another tiny speck in this infinite universe with so many universes, possibly with far greater intelligence than our own which is an admixture of physicality and energy of the supernal and that one remote control called humanity is capable of influencing and directing all of them. The old man raised his fist and said, "I can never accept the literal concept of mind over matter." He was 79 then and, having lost control of his emotions, he was about to hit me. He simply could not bear to hear those words in the Zohar. Nevertheless, those are words and hopefully, with this knowledge, we can achieve the objective of "Love Thy Neighbor" by making people more aware of what the real world is all about. By dedicating ourselves to the dissemination of a more all-embracing harmony in human affairs at the human level, we may learn to care for and understand each other.

3

Astral Influences:
Gamble or Guarantee?

"God does not play dice."

— Albert Einstein

THE IMPORTANCE OF ASTRAL INFLUENCES, STRESSED BOTH BY THE Bible and the Zohar, make it clear that "chance" is no answer to the question of why things happen to us. There are some bizarre coincidences that only astrology can explain. To illustrate the point, let us turn to the Bible and the phrase, "The children of Israel shall pitch by their fathers' houses."[39] Since there is no Hebrew word for "pitch," the word obviously stems from a corruption of translation. The proper translation is, "They shall rest...according to his father's house." What, then, is the significance of a flag? Though ancient in tradition throughout the history of all the world's people, no one ever really has pinpointed the origin of the tradition of the flag, banner or ensign. From a Kabbalistic point of view, the flag means more than just honor and ego, but if the Bible is a spiritual instrument, would the meaning of a flag not also display some form of spirituality?

The word, which is omitted in all translations of the Bible, is the same Hebrew word that appears in Genesis whenever the Bible discusses signs of the seasons, which is to say, signs of the Zodiac. What then, is the relationship, if any, between the concept of the flag, signs of the Zodiac and "according to their father's house?" After asking these questions, the Zohar then states that herein lies the secret of astrology — the internal creation of the signs. Conventional astrology recognizes only the superficial, external energy field force of astral signs and influences. The internal energy center and magnetic fields of the Zodiac are completely forgotten. As the Zohar indicates, "This which was also the aspect that was lost."[41] Conventional astrology, therefore, brings a great number of contradictions, despite providing a great deal of service and insight because somewhere along the line, something has been lost.

This particular chapter of the Zohar indicates that the position of flags and encampments described in the Bible are directly related to the internal magnetic cosmic fields generated by signs of each constellation. It is in these verses that the true astral influences which relate to the positions of the tribes of Israel now are revealed in our generation fully and for the first time. Signs of the Zodiac, symbolized by the tribes, were placed in a position establishing three in each of four directions forming the sides of a rectangle. They represent the four elements of the universe, with the air sign aligned to the east, the water sign to the south, the fire sign to the north and the earth sign to the west.

Thus, a seemingly insignificant passage in the Bible takes on a new depth of meaning which, hopefully, will permit conventional astrology to achieve its proper place among the sciences. Alignment of the tribes, representing elemental signs of the Zodiac, symbolizes Israel's structure as a three-column system with positive and negative poles cosmically balanced by a central pillar. This is the weapon with which Moses took the Israelites out of bondage in Egypt and the power that still accrues to those who pursue and achieve mastery of its secrets, not the least of which is information relative to peoples who live, even now, in the east, west, north and south. By such means are the validity of astrology established.

Astrology combines the worlds of metaphysics and astral in-fluences, the internal aspect of astrology, with the science of astronomy and the physical expression and manifestation of the inter-nal with magnetic energy fields.

The infinite, vast and boundless, darkness is densely packed with infinite points of brightness which ultimately extend into billions of tiny glowing illuminations. These illuminations are themselves com-posed of an infinite number of radian points of light which we know as stars. Why are stars there? Again Zohar I⁴² explains, and in doing so, continues the validation of the influence of astral bodies:

"Hence Solomon, who knew everything, spoke thus: 'Now observe that all of the doings of the world are controlled by vast numbers of astral entities. But the people of the world know not and regard not what is that which upholds them.'⁴³ Even Solomon, wisest of men, could not comprehend them. There is no grass below that does not have an astral spirit or force from above. This blade of grass cannot begin to reap life provided the astral force, a specific star, does not beat it and exclaim, "Now grow!"

Could there be a clearer indication of the importance of astral en-tities? Much greater are the forces of the planets and signs of the Zodiac which are so close to our universe that we cannot help but be influenced by the astral energy fields. For the Jew and the non-Jew alike, religious links seem to be in opposition to the effects of astral in-fluences and the study of astrology. The religious, orthodox-oriented Jew seems to be extremely imbued with this sort of antagonistic at-titude toward astrology — a mindset generally matched by Christian fundamentalists and educated atheists alike, (and if atheism is not a religion, why do its practitioners preach it so fervently?) To these religionists, I would have to ask the same questions that the Zohar poses when it asks why the Jewish nation was born during the astral planetary influence of Mars. Why did the liberation of the Jew, the emancipation from slavery, take place on the 15th day in the sign of the Zodiac of Aries the Ram? Why are particular days chosen to com-memorate and celebrate particular holidays? Is there any reason why the revelation on Mount Sinai occurred during the influence of Gemini? Is it by mere coincidence that the destruction of the Temple commenced during the month of the Zodiac sign of Cancer and culminated it its total destruction during the month of Leo? Why is the first month of the year to be considered during the constellation of the month of Libra?

Ultimately, all people of all faiths will come to the realization that the Jewish Religion is not just that. It is, rather, an instrument defining the universe and its various cosmos. Jewish Holidays are merely a timetable for the comprehension of specific manifestations of cosmic energies.

The practice of following signs of the Zodiac is constantly mentioned in Kabbalistic material. Vast numbers of writings exist concerning the constellations and the galaxy. Why would Hanuka and Purim necessarily take place under the influence of Jupiter, as stated in Kabbalistic writings, or, more particularly, by Rabbi Isaac Luria? When we observe our constellations and their stars and see the structured order that exists in the skies, we then can begin to appreciate the magnitude of our galaxy. Yet, even now, opposition to such studies continues to deprive man of the opportunity, as stated by the Zohar, to know and understand his environment so that he no longer must be a victim of the whims of astral influence. Man is unique and can determine his own destiny, but he cannot expect to accomplish much without the mystical realities of astrology.

Modern man can credit himself with acquiring more knowledge and wisdom than all of his ancestors. He knows there is an interplanetary relationship between the moon and the earth, and yet, for some strange reason, he remains oblivious to the extent of its mystery. Newsweek magazine once ran a front cover depicting a clock, the hands of which pointed to the hours of 5 p.m. and 7 p.m., that time span being the period during which most people fear aggravated robbery, arson and mugging. But why is that period so justifiably feared? Did criminals gather at some point at a convention to decide that the best time for violent crime lay between the hours of 5 and 7? Why has no one suggested that the statistically provable rise in crime as sunset approaches is driven by a cosmic energy force that compels people so inclined to exercise the violence of their greed? The prime example is as old as the Book of Exodus in which, in Moses' absence, built their golden calf late in the afternoon.[45] In this, the astrologer preceded the statistician by three and a half millenia.

Astrology gradually is being recognized as a vehicle of viable, scientific truth encompassing the entire electromagnetic field of our universe. There is growing awareness by scientists that man truly is a responsive element in the cosmos, but the forces that dictate man-inspired events remain largely unseen and unknown. For example, the inexorable pattern of Jupiter and Saturn coincides with the death in office of every American president elected in a zero election year, and some of these presidents even studied the pattern in an effort to break the cycle. The presidential doom factor, however, lies less in the final digit of the election year than in the planetary conjunction that occurred at the time of a president's rise to office. It really all began when William Henry Harrison was elected in 1840. He died of pneumonia in 1841. Twenty years later, in 1860, Abraham Lincoln was elected. He was assassinated in 1865. James A. Garfield was elected in 1880, 20 years after Lincoln won his first term. Garfield was assassinated in 1901. Warren Harding was elected in 1920 and died in office in 1923. In 1940, Franklin D. Roosevelt won his third term and died in office during his fourth term. in 1945. Then came John F. Kennedy, elected in 1960, only to be assassinated in 1963. In each case, these zero-year victors rose to the Oval Office when Jupiter and Saturn were in conjunction, an astral event that occurs every 20 years, but if skeptics still are inclined to snort "mere coincidence," they will be hard-pressed to apply that misunderstood term to the bizarre Lincoln-Kennedy coincidence that stemmed from an un-breakable bond of destiny that spanned more than a century and ir-revocably connected the lives of the two martyred presidents. How can this incredible skein of circumstances be written off by any in-telligent human as random occurrences:

The successors, both of Lincoln and of Kennedy, were southerners named Johnson and both Johnsons had served in the U.S. Senate. Andrew Johnson, Lincoln's successor, was born in 1808 and Lyndon Johnson, who took the mantle from Kennedy, was born in 1908. Lin-coln's assassin was born in 1839 and Kennedy's in 1939. Both assassins were murdered before they could be brought to trial.

Both Lincoln and Kennedy lost children while in the White House. John Wilkes Booth, Lincoln's assassin, shot his victim in a theater and fled to a warehouse. Lee Harvey Oswald shot Kennedy from a warehouse and fled to a theater. The full names of both assassins contain fifteen letters while the names of the succeeding vice presidents each had 13 letters. Both Lincoln and Kennedy were in their early 30s when they married, each to a beautiful 24-year-old brunette, both of whom spoke French fluently. Lincoln had a secretary named Kennedy who advised him not to attend the theater in which he was assassinated. Kennedy had a secretary named Lincoln who urged him not to go to Dallas where he died. Lincoln had a cousin who became a U.S. Senator and another cousin who was mayor of Boston. Another relative, Levi Lincoln, was a Harvard graduate who became U.S. attorney general and Robert Lincoln, the president's son, was minister to London for four years. John F. Kennedy's relatives held similar positions in government. Teddy Kennedy was a U.S. Senator from Massachusetts. Robert Kennedy, also a Harvard graduate, became attorney general, then a U.S. senator from New York. John Kennedy's grandfather was mayor of Boston and his father was ambassador to London. Both Lincoln and Kennedy competed for vice presidential nominations a century apart, in 1856 and 1956, and the presidential campaigns of both were marked by dramatic debates — Lincoln with Stephen A. Douglas and Kennedy with Richard M. Nixon. Both presidents were deeply involved with civil rights for blacks, both were shot in the back of the head in the presence of their wives and both died on Friday.

Such an uncanny series of coincidences involving the lives and deaths of our 16th and 35th presidents cannot be shrugged off lightly or dismissed casually. The powers that propel such things have not changed since they were manifested in Moses' day, which takes us back to the making of the golden calf in Exodus. "And when the people saw that Moses delayed to come down from the mount, the people gathered themselves together unto Aaron and said unto him, 'Make us a god who shall go before us.'"[46]

The word "people," in this case, denotes a mixed multitude including all the sorcerers and magicians of Egypt who followed Moses on the Exodus.[47] "During the day, the wizards practiced their unholy arts from the beginning of the second half of the sixth hour to the commencement of the second half of the ninth hour, while the lesser magicians worked from the middle of the ninth hour until midnight. They did this because during these evening hours certain negative astral influences were in ascendancy. The sorcerers tapped these sources of energy and used them to animate the golden calf." It is with less spectacular results, but with identical motive, that today's criminals, ignorant of what they are doing, take the same evening route to evil, and the same negative cosmic influences have overshadowed the lives of presidents elected in zero years. Kennedy and Lincoln, with a reincarnate link between them, were effectively handed the same program cassette and had little choice beyond some minor restructuring but to live it out.

Can things really happen by chance? There must be some underlying explanation for such bizarre coincidences involving events separated by time and space. Common sense alone would deny that ungoverned chance alone could be responsible for such an interlocking series of events as those that marked the lives of Kennedy and Lincoln a century apart. Correlation, not random chance, alone can be responsible for such a thing.

Science considers this a connecting principle: If A causes B, then A must occur in time before B. Synchronous happenings (syn meaning together and chronous meaning time) occur regularly from year to year and such synchronicity lies at the very heart of the science of astrology. Things that happen through a conjunction of events, whether they take place in time only a moment apart or centuries removed, are intimately connected. Once a contract has been made, that contract continues to influence whether it be a legal document, a manifestation of metaphysics or a scientific axiom.

In the 1920s, Heisenberg discovered that since we cannot measure both the position and the momentum of any object in this universe with exact precision, the very concepts of position and momentum were thrown into doubt. It was a radical change in basic physics that shook the foundation of the scientific community. Heisenberg's uncertainty principle focused attention as never before on the intimate relationship between the observer and the world as we see it. Known as the quantum theory, it forms a basis in what subsequently became known as the age of new physics. It provided the most impressive scientific evidence yet that consciousness plays an essential, if not a deciding role in the nature of physical reality.

All of this originally began with attempts by the scientific world to mechanize the thought processes of logic and reasoning. The ability to reason usually has been claimed to be the single element that distinguishes man from other species. Nevertheless, it often had been considered that reason is a patterned process somewhat governed by conditional laws. When paradoxes pop up so easily in set theory, however, doubt began to taint all of mathematics. Before atomic uncertainty became reality, it was assumed that all material objects obeyed and complied with the laws of mechanics. It was discovered, however, that the atomic world appeared fuzzy and, at times, full of chaos. Particles at that level no longer appeared to follow a well defined trajectory and subatomic particles refused to be pinned down.

Heisenberg's uncertainty principle is the basic ingredient of the whole of quantum mechanics. It takes us directly to the consequences of unpredictability and thus of questionability. Suddenly, it could be seen that events may occur without a cause. Quantum seems to break the causal principle by allowing things to happen with no apparent reason. Scientists now have accepted atomic uncertainty as truly intrinsic to nature.

A distinguished scientist, who unexpectedly turned religionist, voiced his disagreement. The opinion of Albert Einstein and his now famous quote, "God does not play dice with the universe" has little to do with what constitutes reality. To suddenly fall back on so flimsy an argument—that within the divine shall we find our answers—does not seem to fit the description of a scientist. The ensuing debates are scarcely worth mentioning. The centrality of the issue is the daring question as to whether the atom is something or just an abstract construct of our imagination. Maybe it is just a thought, but if so, whose thinking lies behind the effect? If this thing really exists as a separate entity, then at very minimum it should have a definite position and momentum.

To further confuse the issue, the famous Danish physicist Neils Bohr said, "If you don't see it, it isn't there," but surely the world out there exists whether or not we are looking at it. The chair upon which I am sitting may have disappeared, subatomically, but I am not likely to fall upon the floor because of it by confusing the distinction between subject and object, or between cause and effect, we seem strongly to suggest that consciousness, or the mind element, is essential to our observation of the real world. If this is true, however, then the question that must be raised is whether or not the observer and the intelligence necessarily to the act of observation need be human. Will the artificial intelligence of the computer eventually suffice? The question leads us back to the discussion of what and where the mind may be. Does the consciousness have any influence over the physics or chemistry of the corporeal body? The answer is as simple as the law of action and reaction. If the body acts on the mind, then it only follows that the mind acts on the body. Yet from a Kabbalistic point of view, the soul or mind always has the potential ability to govern the internal force of the body that unseen force, the desire to receive for the self alone. Free will is alive and well so, in effect, how can any concept really be given a name? This aspect of uncertainty really means that no matter how accurately one tries to measure the classical quantities of position and momentum, there always will be an uncertainty in the measurement. As Heisenberg observed, predicting the future of atomic particles is impossible under these circumstances.

There is no question that this sort of thinking about cosmos is new to the Western mind. The physicist now discovers that the very act of observing the atomic world introduces a kind of duality; a paradoxical way of seeing things.

Thus, when we consider coincidence separated by time and space, both of which are relative, that coincidence can be true because of astrological positioning. Because of Zodiacal positions and their influence at any time, such strange series of interrelated events as those linking the lives and deaths of Lincoln and Kennedy can occur. As Heisenberg wrote, "The understanding is recognized even before it is rationally understood in detail."

All of this can be thoroughly confusing for the layman, but reference to it is necessary to illustrate how little control we really exercise over our own destinies. More than 30 years ago, George Orwell structured a signpost in our future with his ominous "1984." By that awful date, he postulated that humankind as he knew it in 1943 would have ceased to exist — not in a universal holocaust but in measures far more subtle. Orwell was writing of death without the firing of a single shot; a world populated by people who would go right on living but, since they had stopped thinking, a world in which individual consciousness and free determination no longer would exist. In Orwell's visionary future, the activities of all mankind would conform to and be directed by scientists through manipulation and the government's policy described by the motto, "Big Brother is Watching You."

Orwell was incredibly ingenious in formulating this silent holocaust, but he did not have to invent much of it. He had to look no further than the development of the new age of physics to see his terrible fairy tale and grim prophetic fantasies come to life. The individual seemed to be gradually losing control of himself and his environment. Science, which previously seemed to have provided mankind with total solutions, suddenly was speaking in terms of uncertainty, and today, humankind goes right on fumbling unpredictably in a welter of indeterminism.

A few scientists today insist that changing such programmed behavior is vital to our survival and they go so far as to recommend genetic engineering as an effective means to accomplish it. Increasing numbers of women turn to sperm banks, hoping to be impregnated with the seed of a Nobel Prize winner in the hope that the child they bear may be intellectually gifted. If ever we do learn how to increase intelligence, grant longevity or guarantee other traits providing a competitive advantage through genetic engineering, there will be no shortage of clients prepared to take their place in line. On the dark side, however, those who reject the new technology may find their offspring condemned to subhuman status, there to bear the echo of Adolf Hitler's cruel "untermenchen" brand. From all this automated, roboticized technology may grow a future featuring an underclass of humans so low in status as to seem inferior to the machine. Could it be that as machines evolve their own kind or artificial intelligence that people may become just another, inferior, form?

What seems to emerge from all this is man's inability to advance as quickly as the technology he himself is creating. We are told that our logical faculties arise only after the fact. Things happen long before they are rationally understood. If progress and development seem to point to humankind's inability to control its destiny, then free will vanishes and cosmic determinism well may be part of our inhabited universe. It makes little difference whether the determining entity is science, government or cosmos, the average human will have little, if any, say in the management of his daily affairs. It is almost as if technology is just another extraterrestrial life form directing and dictating human destiny.

One point, however, should be made in favor of cosmic influence. Of the three mentioned, it alone cannot be accused of the dehumanizing and mechanistic aspects which science or government inevitably bring into the equation. While the cosmic effect potentially is more disastrous, it nevertheless is subtle in nature.

Human beings are seen today as little more than complex machines involuntarily caught up in a mammoth mechanistic universe. The future, we feel, already is out there like a great gear train just waiting for our personal cogs to mesh and turn toward already determined conclusions. If such is the case, however, are we really powerless to change it, or does the new physics, with its quantum uncertainty principle, pull the rug out from under our feet and make a strong case for free will which endows the individual with an important role in the nature of physical reality? What, then, is it going to be: Predeterminism or free will? How can we reconcile quantum uncertainty with predetermined astral or cosmic influences? If all things are predetermined, we are placed upon a course of action that has been decided in advance of our existence. The concept of cosmic intelligence seems to exclude our participation in the cosmic plan, whereas the quantum principle undermines cosmic determinism inasmuch as the observer also is a participant.

Let us examine the position of determinism as it is understood by the Kabbalah.

"Why," asks the Zohar, "should there be righteous men who are physical wrecks while many unrighteous men are hale and hearty?"[50]

"One explanation is that the latter were born of righteous parents while the former, though righteous themselves, were not children of righteous parents. The facts, however, militate against this since we see many righteous men who are the sons of righteous parents who nevertheless are afflicted with bodily ills and are lifelong sufferers. There is a deep mystery here because all God's pathways are based on truth and righteousness. In connection with this verse, I have found two mystical doctrines, each of which supports the other, in the books of the ancients. In essence, this is what they proclaim:

There is a period when the moon is defective and judgement is visitied upon her and the sun is hidden from her. It is the moon that, in all times and seasons, releases souls to enter the sons of men, having previously gathered them for that purpose. A soul released during that period when the moon is under sentence — more specifically, when she begins to descend of the 15th day of the lunar month — everyone born at that particular time always will be the victim of degradation, poverty and chastisement whether or not he is sinful or righteous. Those souls which the moon sends forth when she is in the grade of ascencion and completeness and the perennially flowing stream plays upon her are destined to enjoy abundance of all good things, riches, children and bodily health, all on account of the Mazal that flowed forth and joined itself to that grade in order to be perfected and blessed by it."

We thus see, that all things are dependent upon Mazal astral influence by the dictum that "children, life and livelihood" do not depend on man's merits, but on his astral influence, Mazal. Hence, all those who are sorely afflicted in this world, in spite of being truly righteous, suffer through the mischance of their souls."

What we learn from the foregoing Zohar is that the constellations present constant forces in the universe and planets present changing forces. The forces of the constellations almost can be pictured in physical terms as the carriers of the force, modulated by the play of planetary influences, all of which are exerted on the renewal and birth of souls.

Another indication of the link between astrology and science is provided in the Zohar[51] when it discusses eclipses. In this case, the Zohar is concerned with an eclipse of the Moon. If it occurs in the first 15 days of the month in its ascent, the Zohar says, "Because the Moon is a composite of good and evil, it reflects the destinies of both Israel and Ishmael. When the Moon is eclipsed in the time when ascending until she is full, it is an evil sign for Israel. However, when the Moon is eclipsed at the time of its descent, it is an evil omen unto Ishmael." This clearly demonstrates the astral influence of the Moon.

We have further demonstration of the link between astral influences and daily lifestyles in the same Zohar when it says[52], "And God made two great lights." The Zohar then explains that statement: "The word 'made' signifies the due expansion and establishment of the whole. the words 'two great lights' show that at first they were associated as equals. These were invested with greater dignity and they are placed at the head because they derive from on high and ascend for the benefit of the world and for the preservation of worlds. Similarly, the two lights ascended together with the same dignity. The Moon, however, was not at ease with the Sun and, in fact, each felt mortified by the other.

The Moon said, "Where dost thou pasture?"[53]

The Sun said, "Where dost thou make thy flock to rest at noon?[54] How can a little candle shine at midday?"

The Lord thereupon said to her (the Moon), "Go and diminish thyself." She felt humiliated and said, "Why should I be as one that veileth herself," meaning to become diminished.

Whereupon the Lord said, "Go thy way forth in the footsteps of the flock."

Whereupon she diminished herself so as to be the head of the lower ranks. From that time on she has had no light of her own, but derives her light from the Sun.

At first they were equal. Afterwards she (the Moon) diminished herself among all those grades of hers, though she is still head of them. For a woman enjoys no honor save in conjunction with her husband.

It is important, at this point, to cite the recognition of astrology in the Talmud.[60] "Rabbi Shimon Ben Pazi singled out a contradiction between several Biblical verses. One verse said, 'And the Lord made two great lights'[61] and immediately the verse continues, 'the greater light and the lesser light,'

"The Moon said to the Creator, 'Is it possible for two kings to wear one crown? Can I and the Sun rule jointly over this vast universe?' And the Lord responded, 'Then go and make thyself smaller.'

"'But Lord of the universe,' cried the Moon, 'Because I have suggested that which is proper, must I then make myself smaller?' To which the Lord replied, 'Go and thou wilt rule by day and by night.'

"'But what is the value of this?' bemoaned the Moon. 'Of what use is a lamp in broad daylight?' The Lord replied, 'Go! The nation of Israel shall reckon by thee the days and the years.'

"'But it is impossible,' replied the Moon, 'to do without the Sun for the reckoning of the seasons as it is said, 'And let them be for signs and for seasons and for days and for years.'[55] And the Lord continued, 'Go! The righteous shall be named after thee. Inasmuch as you are made smaller, the righteous shall be called small.'"

Thus we find Jacob the Small[56], Samuel the Small[57] and others.

"Upon seeing that it would not be consoled, the Holy One, the Lord, said, 'Bring an atonement for Me, for making the Moon smaller.'"

This beautiful and intriguing confrontation between the Moon and the Lord is the basis of an incredible Zoharic conclusion. Herein lies the Kabbalistic secret of why we use the lunar-solar system to calculate the year as opposed to the solar system which is the basis of the contemporary Western calendar: "'And the Lord said unto Abraham. Go out from your land and from your birthplace and from the house of your father.'"[58] That commandment, according to the Zohar, told Abraham to leave the house of the Moon, the house of Saturn and the house of Mars, for when the house of Mars, the house of Saturn and the Moon rule, it is said that one never should venture into some new undertaking on the second day of the week, which is Monday, or the fourth day of the week, which is Wednesday. This, according to the Zohar, is because Mars has the heat and redness of the Sun. Purgatory was created and brought forth on the second day of the days of creation. The astrological influence of Mars on that particular day therefore is one of extreme negativity. The original source of energy that produced Purgatory was of a negative quality.

The Moon consists of both good and bad. When she is full, she is considered good, but in her descending stage she is evil. As a result, as an astral influence, she will shine negatively on the fourth day because on the fourth day the Moon reduced the energy field she originally was created with. Subsequently, the Moon came to be known as impoverished and in time of her descent negative energies pervade the universe."[59]

Of all the verses in the Bible, these particular passages in the Talmud and in the Zohar carry with then the entire idea of Kabbalistic astrology. It is by far the most profound, most ancient and most widely held concept in Kabbalah. These two passages reveal the whole system of astrology. From them we can learn the very essence of our universe and the very essence of the astral influences which completely envelop and, unfortunately at times, control the destiny of man. The implications of these passages are profound and sweeping. They demand tremendous change in our present theories of astronomy and concepts of the whole spectrum of astrology.

What emerges from the foregoing Zohar and Tractate Hulin is the Hebrew astrologer's view of the astral influence of planets and constellations, their views being very different from those of contemporary astrologers. Sun sign astrology is the extent of what most people consider to be all there is to know about astrology. A Kabbalist will tell you this is a long way from the in-depth astrological knowledge inasmuch as external cosmic astral influences are only the manifestations and physical expressions of multi-changing forces and resulting interactions of the relationships between them. This is over and above the compelling need to know the internal subatomic cosmic energy field of each celestial body which participates in this beautiful, magnificent cosmic production.

There is another point, stressed time and time again, which continues to elude many who seek in-depth energy patterns in observation of the universe. From the Kabbalistic viewpoint, behavioral patterns of celestial bodies are merely reflections of some internal cosmic intelligence that compels the particular celestial body to behave and move in its peculiar path.

When we ask why there is day and night or why there are 365 days in the year, the conventional answer is that the Earth has two main movements: It rotates on its axis, creating day and night by causing the Sun to appear to move from east to west, and it makes a complete circuit of the Sun in 365 days. The Kabbalist's question, however, is not directed at the physical manifestation of either the Earth's rotation or its journey around the Sun. The Kabbalist asks what peculiar cosmic intelligence force creates this particular physical expression of the earth and its inter-relationship with the Sun. Why must there be a day and night? Why does a gravitational force exist to assure the earth's journey around the Sun in the annual span of 365 days? Why does each season last approximately 91 days? The reader of Kabbalistic material must start to ask such questions, but to think in this manner requires a new process and compels a bit of re-thinking. This new age of physics requires a completely new, revolutionary approach to the way in which we view the universe. The aspiring Kabbalist must begin to ask this sort of question because to think in this fashion requires a new intellectual process and mandates a bit of re-thinking. This new age of physics requires a completely new and revolutionary approach to the way we view the universe.

Early Kabbalists were familiar with the internal cosmic fields of celestial bodies and regarded observed movements across the heavens as physical expressions of the interplay of cosmic extraterrestrial intelligence. They viewed each constellation and planet as an entity in which the constant forces of the four elements—water, fire, air and earth—were operative. Their observations of the universe, drawn from the various source reflections of the Zohar, enabled them to provide a valid guide for the individual in his search for a total understanding of self. Furthermore, and more importantly, they provided a discipline for human and moral behavior, taking the individual to a higher level of consciousness and consequently to a higher level of moral conduct.

The Sun and Moon exert the most direct influence over earth's inhabitants along with the astral influences of the main planetary bodies, Jupiter, Mars, Saturn, Venus and Mercury. After passing these difficult obstacles, we find the whole of our universe amazingly simple and clear — so amazingly simple and clear that we initially will be prompted to ask, "Why have I never seen it that way?"

There never can be a better world until there are better people in it. When individuals reflect upon themselves and their own particular, unique misery, the important thing to consider is a better means for achieving major changes and the aleviation of some of the basic problems that confront us all. The enlightenment presented in this book previously has been the preserve of a mere handful of sages, mystics, prophets and holy people who, through reaching upper levels of cosmic consciousness while still in the flesh, have seen man and the universe as they really are in all their beauty.

Unfortunately, science has all but done away with individual value. Man now is part of a functioning unit. By compiling all the known facts and figures concerning man, we then computerize him and extrude a model of behavior which excludes any personal uniqueness or identity. Progress reduces us to a numerical entity — a credit card which we take great care in preserving, at times, at the expense of individual identity. Through astrology, the individual becomes aware of his internal intelligent cosmic force. In astrology there is only a recognition of the weak and strong characteristics that make up an individual. From Aries to Pisces, these ideas are generally known and they provide the individual with a tool with which he better can discover himself. The internal knowledge of astrology, which was lost and yet concealed in the Book of Formation, stressed the point that whenever any movement in the music of the universe is noted, there is some internal metaphysical force that has brought it about to be sensed and, at times, actually seen.

Thus, in recounting the dialogue between the Sun, the Moon and the Lord, the Zohar makes the point that the reason the Sun has less influence upon the Moon at times when the Moon begins to disappear is because the negative, left column influence of the Moon becomes more dominant following the 15th day of the new Moon. This brings about the descent of the Moon. Conversely, at the beginning of the new lunar month we observe the Moon in an ascending postion. What we experience then, and what the internal astral influence indicates, is the constant rise of the all inclusive positive energy force or a gradual revealment of this energy. This is the physical relationship between the Sun and the Moon.

It appears self evident that the predictive nature of astral influences seem to dictate the progression and environment of man. How, then, can we reconcile the concept that astrology is not fatalistic? How do we reconcile Kabbalistic astrology with the destiny of man when that supposedly is in his own hands?

In anticipation of this question, the Zohar[62] answers: "I dwell with him that is of a contrite and humble spirit, to revive the heart of the contrite ones."[63] Elsewhere, the Zohar expands the theme: "Behold, the Creator is close to those of a broken heart."[64] These are verses which refer to those who are fellow sufferers with the Moon in her defect and regarding whom it is fitly said, 'To revive the heart of the contrite ones.' That is, to make those who participated in the suffering of the Moon participate in the new life to be bestowed on her in the future. Such sufferings undergone by them are called sufferings in a token of love. And prayer is the method by which the souls can be renewed with the renewal of each Moon."

In short, while a fixed position is placed upon every individual, there still are choices he can make by which the element of distress can be removed. He can, if he wishes, transcend any position in which he finds himself by means of meditation and prayer. This is amplified in Zohar I:[65] "Hence Solomon, who knew everthing, spoke thus: 'I observe that all of the vast doings of the world are controlled by vast numbers of spirits, but the people of the world know not and regard not what it is that upholds them."[66] Even Solomon, the wisest of men, could not comprehend them. He further states: 'He had made everything beautiful in its time; also set the world in their heart, so that man cannot find the works that God had done.'[67] Whatever the Creator has formed in the world has its own controlling grade that directs it either for good or for evil. There are grades of the right and grades of the left and neither is evil unless it is out of balance with its counterpart. If a man goes to the right, then whatever he does becomes a directing grade on that side. This helps him on and procures other helpers. But if he goes to the left, then whatever act he commits becomes a directing force on that side. This, in turn, brings indictments against him while leading him further into that side.

Thus, whenever a man performs a good and proper act, the chieftain of the right side affords him help. This is indicative of the expression, "good in its time," in which the act and its time become infinitely bound up together, and "he has set the world in their heart," which means the whole world and all its works depend *solely on the will* of man. Happy are those righteous who, by their good deeds, draw benefits upon themselves and upon the world. They know how to attach themselves to the grade called time of peace. By virtue of their righteousness in the lower world, they influence the upper world."

Thus it may be seen that everything in the universe is dependent upon man's free will. As it is written, "So that man cannot find out the works that God has done from the beginning, even to the end." Inasmuch as it depends upon man's will whether his deeds are attached to the proper grade or to the improper one, the text continues, "I know that there is no good in them but to rejoice and to perform good actions so long as they live."[68]

If a man's actions are not good, he has to rejoice at all of the consequences however grim they may be. He should give thanks and do good actions as long as he lives. Even if his own acts have brought evil upon him through the grade that he, himself, initiated, he still must rejoice at the consequences and give thanks for them because he brought them on himself like a bird blindly falling into a snare. Such consequences, willingly, if unconsciously, sought, are for tikune purposes and therefore are advantageous, even in pain. Self pity offers no advantage.

The Zohar[69] spells this out: "For man also knoweth not his time; as the fishes that are taken in an evil net, and the birds that are caught in a snare, even so are the sons of men snared in an evil time, when it has fallen suddenly upon him."[70]

The expression "in his time" refers to the ministering angel for that particular cosmic energy force called time who presides over each act a man performs. It is referred to in the statement: "He had made everything beautiful in its time. They are as the birds that are caught in the snare. Happy are those who exert themselves in the study of the Torah and are intimate with the ways and paths of the Torah so as to follow the true path."

The coded message we have received from the Zohar is that basically there are 28 astral periods of time: 14 good and 14 bad, as stipulated. There are 14 positive and 14 negative times throughout the year. The Zohar here is revealing the secret doctrine that these 14 times will move man with cosmic energy in the direction that man, himself, has chosen. If man's action is positive, he can direct at the very same time, the positive aspect. If he moves in a negative direction, he then initiates what we might consider the button that activates the negative column. While the forces of cosmic energy and time do prevail and do control our universe, we nevertheless can draw from this Zohar the truth that man still is at the helm of the boat.

And to man has been given this vast knowledge that previously had been concealed, even to King Solomon the Wise. This knowledge is revealed to us by the Book of Formation and its subsequent profound commentary, the Book of Splendor—the Zohar.

"To everything there is a season and a time to every purpose under the heavens. A time to be born and a time to die; a time to plant and a time to pluck up that which was planted. A time to kill and a time to heal; a time to break down and a time to build up. A time to weep and a time to laugh; a time to mourn and a time to dance. A time to cast away stones and a time to gather stones together; a time to embrace and a time to refrain from embracing. A time to get and a time to lose; a time to keep and a time to cast away. A time to rend and a time to sew; a time to keep silence and a time to speak. A time to love and a time to hate; a time of war and a time of peace."[71]

We have spoken of 28 astral influences—14 on the positive side and 14 on the negative. These 28 "times," all cited in this lovely verse from Ecclesiastes are energy forces which, from a Kabbalistic viewpoint, can be intimately known and predicted so that the individual will be prepared to take advantage of them when they occur. They are cosmic nerve centers just waiting to be put to good use. It is also noteworthy that all astral influences are based on the cosmic energy centers of the seven planets which are related to the four basic elements of water, fire, air and earth. These seven planets, multiplied by the four elements of which they consist, again repeat the coded number — 28.

4

Cosmic Wanderers

Is the universe created or external?
It behooves us to point out the great difficulty of this
investigation. For by being aware of the difficulty of a problem,
we are guided to the way which leads us to the attainment
of the truth thereof.

— Gersonides

NE CANNOT CONCLUDE A DISCUSSION OF ASTRAL IN-
fluences without paying due respect to that most mysterious and
myth-laden of them all — the comet. For centuries, appearances of
these solar wanderers have been greeted with awe, apprehension
and, as with so many other celestial phenomena, complete
misunderstanding.

About all that is certain, even today, about a comet is that it is a
heavenly body consisting of a nucleus and a tail that extends to vast
length across the sky as it revolves about the sun. Comets usually are
distinguished from other members of the solar system by their diffuse
appearance and the character of their orbits which generally are elip-
tical and enormous. There are, however, some comets with orbits
that so closely resemble those of some of the minor planets that

distinction becomes almost impossible. Since comets (Halley's excepted) appear at irregular intervals and move in a rapid and unpredictable fashion, they long have been regarded with mingled interest and fear.

Since mankind long has assumed that heavenly bodies exercise some control over the affairs of men, it is only natural that they once were regarded with considerable suspicion. They have become associated with omens of disaster, often foretelling the overthrow of kings and nations. The famed Bayeux tapestry portraying the Norman Conquest of England in 1066 features Halley's comet as a most terrifying object, and while it certainly may have been an ill omen for the Saxon king who died at the Battle of Hastings with an arrow through his eye, it certainly bode no ill for William the Conquerer.

Comets are rebellious members of our solar system, appearing to obey none of the normal rules of the cosmic road. The planets all move in the same direction around the sun while comets move with equal frequency in either direction. The orbits of the planets are nearly circular and lie very closely in the same plane. The orbit of a comet is very elongated and may lie along any plane.

Where comets originate remains a scientific mystery to this very day. Astronomers have postulated an "Oort cloud," far beyond the orbit of Pluto, in which they may be born, but little empirical evidence of its existence has been found. The scientific community prefers to avoid the ever-pressing Kabbalistic question as to why they appear at all because, without a ready answer, that question always is an embarrassment. The fact remains, however, that we probably know less about the origin of the comets than about any other object in cosmos. Theories postulated since man began to view the heavens have shed little light upon the subject. Ideas of the mode of origin of the comets are as numerous as the innumerable astronomers who have studied them.

Despite the fact that substantial progress has been made on the problem, definite answers are not available. Generally accepted notions have had to be revised routinely in the light of new, advanced, high tech into the frontier of space, but convincing arguments generally have led to the rather generally held conclusion that comets always have been members of our solar system, but information suggesting that they may have originated somewhere in the interstellar region of our universe no longer is rejected out of hand.

Since the mystery continues, once again we must advance the Kabbalistic formula for a true understanding and ask, "Why?" While available evidence reflects upon, and ultimately may have bearing on cometary origins, the Kabbalistic method leaves little room for error.

Rather than start from the present and work backward, as the scientists do, the approach of the Kabbalah is to begin at the beginning and proceed with the creative process down to the present. A good starting point for our investigation is the Hebrew name for a comet. In the wisdom of the Kabbalah, the Hebrew letters and words are coded for the revelation of energy intelligence. Consequently, the Hebrew name for "comet" should reveal its origin and intended energy intelligence force.

Surprisingly enough, the Hebrew word, Shavit, has an Aramaic counterpart, Sharvit. For an interpretation of this significance, let us turn to the Zohar.

"Rabbi Isaac opened a discourse on the verse: 'And the remnant of Jacob shall be in the midst of many peoples as dew from the Lord, as showers upon the grass, that are not looked for from men, nor awaited at the hands of the sons of men.'[72] 'Observe,' he said, 'that every day, as soon as day breaks, a certain feminine (negative) cosmic force awaits her masculine mate for the cosmic connection to reveal the light of day that emanates from the Garden of Eden. Upon receiving the force of the three column energy system Sharvit rules (Shavit) as a scepter in maintaining balance in the universe.'"[73]

What seems to emerge from the Zohar is the mystery of the internal force of a comet. It is the energy force of the three column system whipping (Shavit) the universe into shape. For this very reason, the Hebrew month of Aquarius is Shevat, indicating the advent of the Messiah along with its blessing of "Peace on earth, good will toward one's fellow man."

How is this all going to come about? The Torah is very clear when it declares, "I see it, but not now shall it come to pass. I behold it, but it is not nigh. There shall come a star (the influence of the Z'eir

Anpin, the three column system and a scepter (Shavit) shall rise out of Israel and shall smite the corners of Moab and destroy all the foundation thereof."[74]

Coincidently, the numerical value of Shevat is 311, corresponding to the Hebrew word for Ish (man).[75] The preceding verse points us to the concept surrounding the coming of the Messiah as stated, "And now, behold, I shall go unto my people: come therefore and I will advise thee what this people shall do to thy people at the end of days."[76]

While the comprehension of the star of Shavit was known to the Kabbalists of the Zohar, the sages of the Talmud were not as certain. "Rabbi Samuel said, 'The orbits of the heavens are known to me as the streets of my city Nahardaya. The star of Shavat, however, is not understood.'"[77]

Consequently, the Kabbalistic interpretation of a comet is regarded as an omen of freedom and balance, rather than as an omen of disaster. The comet's tail represents the energy intelligence of the Vav of the Tetragrammaton. Therefore, its appearance is as a tail similar to the letter Vav, which portrays a rod or stick. The front round, or face, of the comet symbolizes the mating of Malkhut with the Vav or the positive energy intelligence of the Vav, with the negative energy intelligence of Malkhut, creating the unified circuit of energy. The effect of this mating is balance and stability.

The conclusion of what has just been said raises a serious question. Is the tail the result of the head, or nucleus, of the comet as it appears to us, or the other way around? From a Kabbalistic point of view, the Vav preceeds the Hay, or Malkhut (negative energy intelligence) as its position in the Tetragrammaton. Thus, while the telescope or naked eye seems to observe the tail as being formed of molecules and dust particles driven out from the coma, indicating the coma came first and the tail second, Kabbalistically, it is the other way around, just as the true influence of a comet, as perceived by mankind through the centuries, is the other way around. Welcome the arrival of a comet. Potentially, it bears only the best!

5

Beyond the Test Tube

"To see a world in a gram of sand,
And a heaven in wild flower,
Hold infinity in the palm of your hand,
And eternity in an hour."

—William Blake, *Auguries of Innocence*

T HE DAWN OF TRUE SCIENCE, WHEN FREEDOM TO PURSUE OPEN and honest inquiry into cosmos finally emerged from centuries of suffocating superstition and church dogma, came in 1543 when Nicholas Copernicus proclaimed that the Earth and her sister planets revolved around the Sun. Copernicus probably concluded his studies as early as 1530, but given the tenor of the times and the church's predilection for consigning "heretics" to the Inquisitional bonfire, he prudently delayed publication until he was on his death bed. Prior to Copernicus, the Sun, Moon, planets and stars revolved around the Earth by papal decree, and to argue with that sort of proclamation was a dangerous business.

Ironically, astrology now stands where Copernicus stood 400 years ago while "pure" science joins modern religionists in the role of the

16th Century church. Science, ignoring the demands of its own methodology, not only scoffs at astrology's claims, but bluntly refuses even to examine them, while most Jews, including their leaders, still perceive astrology as something alien to Judaism. Most Christian churches go so far as to brand it a work of Satan. The concept of "heresy," unfortunately, lives on, but as in Copernicus' day, its truth will succumb neither to threat nor to decree.

Still, the study and practice of Kabbalistic astrology should not be taken lightly. Its purpose goes far beyond the superficial banter of the singles bar ("Hi there, what's your sign?") and the phenomena it explores prompt caution. They point to a non-materialization of the space/time continuum and warn that the metaphysical unconscious really can cast a great deal of doubt on any naive or hasty explanation of the parallels between the celestial and terrestrial universes; between the metaphysical astral influences of the world beyond and the physical world as we see it. Kabbalistic astrology probes the very nature of reality.

To fully assess astrological phenomena, one must take into account all the other phenomena with which we come into contact. No longer, in light of space exploration and other new dimensions, can we ignore the existence of the metaphysical astral influence that astrology documents. Hopefully, through a little more clarification of the very basic Talmudic studies to which I already have referred, we can move ahead into the area of such phenomena, anticipating the astral intelligences will be very real and logical, if at times, seemingly irrational. Kabbalistic astrology comes to grips with the unknown far more than physicists can, even with their new-found uncertainty principle.

Experimentation once was an attempt to study a system through analysis based on controlled stimulation. This exploration then was followed by observation of the resulting response. Ever since the uncertainty principle, however, controlled experiments on a cosmic level never can be accurately determined. We come to realize the role that theory and ideas play in the discovery of each new physical and cosmic phenomenon. Most cosmic phenomena have surfaced only recently, principally through the introduction into astronomy of new detection techniques. It is only natural to wonder how much more remains unrecognized. Furthermore, technological advances already have uncovered so many new physical and cosmic features that one can only speculate what further refinements may reveal.

The dilemma of observational experiments following the acceptance of the uncertainty principle have raised some grave doubts, since the experiment and the observer no longer are firmly connected. Astronomy fundamentally is an observational science. Present technology is insufficiently advanced to permit physical exploration of the universe beyond the solar system. The distances that must be overcome are simply too enormous. Our most sophisticated robot probes become functionally useless the minute they cross the orbit of Pluto and plunge for eons into the void that stretches between one tiny star in our galaxy and the next nearest one, and so vast is the distance to the next galaxy that physical travel across it may never even be attempted. Since the science of astronomy is so dependent upon observation, it is relatively simple to appraise the impact of required techonological advances as so complex as to verge upon the impossible.

In astronomy, the observer either can choose to detect and analyze signals from extraterrestrial sources or simply ignore them. He has no way of provoking a cosmic source to change its emission. He can only observe that which is brought to his attention, relying on the information carriers such as satellites and radio telescopes that transmit all the astronomer ever will learn about the universe. These transmissions are infinite in nature. Most of the information currently known about extraterrestrial phenomena has been transferred to us by means of radio waves, infrared radiation, cosmic ray particles and other vehicles so minute that they practically cease to exist in reality as we know it. For the present, no magic of technology can help us detect waves that never reach Earth. Science can only help the astronomer reach the known boundaries imposed by the physical universe itself. The ultimate limitations of astronomical information presently are incomplete and attempts to provide a prescription or tentative assessment concerning the number of remaining unrecognized phenomena is pure folly. Thus, results of calculations by theoretical astrophysicists seem almost an exercise in futility, and there already is an uneasy feeling among leading scientists that long-range predictions on the progress of science are doomed to failure. Thus do the most enlightened scientists, unwilling to confer legitimacy upon any study that ventures beyond materiality, lock themselves into the medieval absolutism against which Copernicus fought.

In 1902, a mere five years before he would become the first American scientist to win a Nobel prize, Albert A. Michelson wrote: "The more important fundamental laws and facts of physical sciences have all been discovered. These are now so firmly established that the possibility of their ever being supplanted in consequence of new discoveries is exceedingly remote."[78]

Then, as today, most scientists were so confident in their own understanding of nature that they usually were unwilling to admit the possibility of further revolutionary phenomena or startling discoveries. Here is another example of how the scientific spirit resembles the dogma of religion. Walter Meissner, a colleague of the famous physicist and Nobel prize winner Max Planck, recalls the following story concerning young Planck's choice of his subsequent field of endeavor in preparation for entry into the University of Munich.

"At first, he was uncertain whether to select classical philology, music or physics," Meissner wrote. "He finally decided on physics; This in spite of the fact that the then professor of physics at the University of Munich, Phillip Jolly, advised him against it since (said Jolly) in the field of physics, there was nothing new to be discovered." Some 25 years later, Planck provided the approach to the quantum theory of physics. He was to set down the basic principles for investigative research of atomic and subatomic universes.

In conclusion, the variety of observations we can undertake to explore is finite, due to the infinite potential observations that seem eternally to remain concealed. The behavior of the transmitters of information and the contents of the cosmic container together limit the scope of our observations. Where, therefore, can science or the astrophysist go from here? One way to gain some perspective on the nature of cosmic phenomena is to read what the Kabbalist has to say.

His claim to the information as to how the cosmic universe got started in the first place is as close to its content as we might want to achieve.

The problem of cosmic origin is truly baffling. One can imagine analyzing the seed of a tree, then, upon seeing the tree itself, know that the secrets of the tree lie hidden with another, similar, seed. The universe itself, however, does not furnish us with the seed or blueprint of our observable universe, so one must imagine some bootstrap process that essentially began with nothing. The Sefer Yetzirah, the Book of Formation, along with its commentaries, does just that. We no longer have to content ourselves with a sense of wonder and awe of the heavens. They provide us with answers as to the origin of cosmic life.[80]

The restriction brought about the creative process referred to by the Kabbalist as the emanation of the ten essential energy intelligences (Sefirot). The restriction, the Big Bang itself, at first became manifested as extraterrestrial thought energy intelligences. "Sof Ma'seh, B'Mahshava Tehila," the final act first becomes manifest as thought, declares the famed kabbalist, R. Shlomo Alkabetz.[81]

Following the evaluation of the entire creative thought process, the thought process of the "Big Bang" subsequently became manifest as a material external entity, similar to the internal energy intelligence which became enclothed within a corporeal body. The Tractate Nedarin says "Put aside your foolishness. . .Israel is not under planetary influence."[82] This does not concern the validity of astrology in its application to Abraham and Israel, but rather to Israel as retainer of the secrets of cosmic extraterrestrial intelligence . With proper use, Israel is not and never will be subject to these astral planetary influences. Does this imply existence of the ability to alter cosmic influence at its source? Can man really act on matter in defiance of the fundamental principles of physics? Are there indeed separate laws that govern our universe, a universe where there is no room in the physical process for free will and another in which the entire cosmos must comply with and is dependent upon the behavior of man? It has been suggested that the Quantum Theory, with its involvement of the individual in its very essence, opens the door to the dependency of man's behavior. The accepted doctrine of a deterministic universe, omitting the central figure of this multifaceted reality, seems to be swept away by the quantum factor. That is the matter with which the Talmud deals when it exclaims, "Israel is not under planetary influences."

One more source confirms that statement and, unfortunately, gives ammunition to those who would forbid Jews to study astrology today. To quote from the Tractate Pesahim:[83] 'Rabbi Bar Hanah said in the name of Rabbi Samuel Ben Marta, on the authority of Rabbi Josi of Hutzal, 'How do you know that you must not consult astrologers because it is said, 'Thou shalt be wholehearted with the Lord.' To add more weight to the argument that astrology in some way implies that we have no trust in the Creator, idol worshippers are referred to as worshippers of the stars, obviously indicating that anything connected in any way with astrology can be considered a display of disbelief in the Lord and belief in the deity of the stars. Another major section further strengthening the concept that astrology is something to be avoided is found in a section of the Talmud,[84] "Rabbi Hanina said, 'The planetary influence provides wisdom; the planetary influence also provides wealth. Israel is subject to astral influence. Rabbi Johanan said, 'Israel is not subject to the constellations.' Rabbi Johanan told how we know that Israel is not subject to planetary influence: 'Because it is written, 'Thus saith the Lord, Learn not the ways and customs of the nations and be not dismayed at the signs of the heavens for the nations are dismayed. They are dismayed, but not Israel.' "[85]

The position that Israel is not under planetary influence has become so grounded in Judaic culture that respectable leaders draw their own conclusions no matter how much evidence might be to the contrary.

Various other references, however, indicate that there are astral influences and that we, Israel included, are governed by them. How long will we continue to reject astrology as one of the Creator's creations, made manifest on the fourth day of creation, when He declared that the larger light should rule by day and the lesser light by night? The Judaic position is similar to that of scientists who still hold the belief that our universe and all that it contains arose and developed by chance alone. The reason many accept this is because it provides a great deal of comfort to the individual and to others who do not want to be subject to a ruler, even if He rules the universe. Once this sort of position is taken, the individual really believes himself to be free, but he still will be influenced by these forces, whatever he believes. Astral influences are there and, like the Law of Gravity, they will not go away on the basis of disbelief. The religionist especially delights in debating the question of astrology because it can be turned into a Bible controversy. For the non-religious, who have been raised in a world where free will and free thinking are considered truth, the Bible is nothing more than a compilation of ethical dimensions. He has been molded by Western science and Western philosophy, and while astrology is not foreign to him, he seldom looks beyond the superficial. For the traditionalist, however, who still adheres to the old principles, we hopefully will provide some form of understanding, some logical insight and show him that astrology is dichotomous neither to science nor religion.

In sharp contrast with the controversy between the Rabbis as to whether or not Israel is subject to astral influences, several other readings from the Zohar and the Talmud provide clear illustration that astral influences do exist, and that almost everything depends upon them. In the Talmud, Raba said, "Length of life, children and sustenance, does not depend on merit alone, but on Mazal, the constellation."[86] Zohar I says, "And Avram saw with his wisdom of the stars that he shall not have a son. And consequently it is written, 'And the Lord asked Avram to go outside.'"[87] With this, the Lord was doing more than merely calling Avram outside his home. He was telling him not to feel enslaved by the wisdom of the stars, saying "for you shall have a son."[88] This tells us that Abraham did have knowledge of the stars. He knew the science of astrology, but was told not to feel compelled by them.

Rabbi Akiva was told by astrologers that his daughter was destined to die on her wedding night. This precognition was a continuing source of pain up to and including the night of his daughter's marriage. Gloom and dread dominated the evening as friends and family waited for the inevitable to occur. But as his daughter entered the wedding hall, she removed her hat and, to hang it, thrust its attached pin into a wall separator prepared for the women. The evening passed without incident and the guests left with gladdened hearts, saying that Satan had been thwarted. When the bride removed her hat from the wall, however, she noticed that the pin carried a drop of blood at its tip. Investigating the far side of the wall, she found a dead snake, its eye pierced by the pin she had thrust through the wall.

"What did you do to turn your destiny around?" her father asked her, and she replied, "A poor man came to the door in the evening during the ceremony and festivity and everybody was busy at the banquet and there was none to attend him, so I took the portion that was given to me and gave it to him."

"You have done a good deed," Said Rabbi Akiva, "and you have been delivered from death. Not only from an unnatural death, but from death itself."

This story shows that the knowledge of astrology, from Abraham's time onward, was widespread and widely accepted. Astrologers obviously were very respected in the Jewish community. What emerges from the story of Abraham is an astrological prediction that he never would have a son with Sarah because of an active astral influence. In the case of Rabbi Akiva's daughter, death had been predicted, but thwarted by her own action at the last minute. Abraham, of course, did have a child with Sara, because of a name change, to be discussed in detail later, that altered his astrological chart. In both cases, a statement found repeated many times in the Zohar is affirmed: While the stars impel, they do no compel.

The Zohar states that Abraham was the first known astrologer. He knew the sciences of astrology and astronomy alike and it is to him that authorship of the Book of Formation is attributed, and it is at this point that we can separate Western scientific tradition from the Kabbalistic view of the universe. From Newton's time on, the classical physicist felt he could, in principle, predict with absolute precision the evolution of the universe for all time to come. This mechanistic view of the human mental process precluded any possibility of human free will in the process. The same, however, might be said of astrology. In principle, there can be a prediction of universal evolution that is made with complete precision and absolute detail, but the Kabbalistic perspective also is concerned with man's mortal accountability for his actions because the Kabbalist knows that man's actions can alter the state of the universe. He is not merely an observer who creates reality; he actually determines ultimate results and thus has ultimate responsibility.

•

When physicists try to glimpse the universe at birth to see how primordial material evolved, they somehow impose their own view of reality, which theoretical physicist, Heisenberg aptly named, "The Uncertainty Principle." At Cern, the European high-energy physics center in Geneva, Switzerland, they hope to recreate conditions they *believe* — in the same sense that orthodox religionists believe — existed briefly after the explosive birth of the universe.

Particles forming the nuclei of all atoms are *believed* to consist of sub-atomic particles called quarks bound together by gluons. The latter, they *believe*, may not only form the glue that holds everything together, but may also be agents that bind together the nuclear particles themselves. This has led to *speculation* that under the extraordinary pressure and temperature that existed for a trillionth of a second after the Big Bang, the universe was formed entirely of freely moving quarks and gluons. Anticipating this revelation, physicists are attempting to recreate the conditions extant at the beginning of the universe by initiating the most powerful collisions of sub-atomic particles ever produced in a laboratory.

The least we can expect from such a wacky pursuit is their admission that this kind of hit-and-miss investigative approach is no more valid, and probably less so, than that of the kabbalist, who asserts that he knows the exact conditions extant at the time of the Big Bang, and that he also understands the cause and motivation that brought the Big Bang into existence.

Despite probing by generations of physicists, insight into the internal workings of the atomic nucleus is still imperfectly understood — and will undoubtedly remain so until such time as science begins to view nature from a fresh perspective. The kabbalistic view of the universe, proposing that mankind is not only a participator but a determinator of all energy activity, involves radical changes in the traditional concepts of space and time.

At one time, even in recent memory, technology was regarded as the unlimate problem-solver and the concept of Progress was considered to be the cure for all of man's ills. By rejecting outright man's position and importance within the cosmos, science has caused a significant shift in the values of large segments of the general population, from one of inner personal development to economic and technological concerns.

The principles of Newtonian physics still maintain a strong influence on Western scientific thinking, as many scientists continue to cling to this outdated mechanistic paradigm — this in spite of the quantum theory which posits the intimate relationship between human consciousness and the physical world.

Consequently, seeking the path of least resistance, while still having to admit to man's participation in the establishment of reality, they stop short of the kabbalistic concept that mankind's role within the universe might also be that of "determinator."

•

From the kabbalistic point of view the universe exists in a definitive and never-changing state. Change is a condition only experienced in the physical world. The real world is eternal and Infinitely still. According to Kabbalah, ninety-nine percent of what we normally perceive as "reality" is an illusion. The illusion is comprised of all of life's uncertainties, fragmentation, and all that varies — in short everything that has to do with the physical world — whereas reality never changes.

The world of matter must comply with the illusionary laws of physics which, on the macroscopic level (e.g. ignoring quantum) are mechanical and deterministic. These laws seem to appear incompatible with free will.

Can the consciousness somehow reach into the physical world and create changes in defiance of the fundamental principles of physics? No, says the Kabbalist.

One merely has to reflect on human activity to suspect that some mad metaphysical scientist is on the loose. In fact, according to Kabbalah, the tumult of physical existence was actually placed on earth for the specific purpose of allowing man free will sufficient to alleviate

Bread of Shame — a concept which will be herein explained. This concept of relative free will can assist us in transcending the notion of personal isolation and give amazing insights into our intimate connection with the all-embracing cosmos.

It is to this unity to which the kabbalist aspires.

The capability of changing destiny by what we know as human free will does not necessarily contradict the mechanistic world view of our universe. The trick is to reach another dimension and change what might have been a predictable picture. By achieving an altered state of consciousness, the predictability of the mechanistic view of our universe no longer applies.

Actually, this is not so esoteric as it may sound. The phenomenon of the Black Hole, a collapsed star so dense and so powerful in its gravitational pull that not even light can escape it, is one example of an altered state of physical consciousness. DNA, the physical blueprint of everything that lives, is another. We shall examine both, then attempt to apply their principles to the nonmaterial, metaphysical, alteration of consciousness the Kabbalist seeks as a means of changing what might appear to be an immutable destiny. As the astronomer probes the Black Hole with various radio waves to learn more about its structure and as the geneticist performs surgery on genes to alter the creature they are designed to produce, the Kabbalist will approach the matter through prayer, meditation and often little more than a change of name to alter his astrological chart and with it, his destiny. The scientist journeys through space, interstellar or interatomic, to achieve his purpose. The Kabbalist journeys through time.

Black Holes represent for the physicist the ultimate unknown, and possibly, the unknowable, in science. They constitute an edge or boundary of space/time in which matter and cosmic influences enter or leave the physical universe in a totally unpredicatable manner. Some cosmologists believe the universe emerged, without cause, from just such a primeval naked singularity which is the closest concept science has found to a paranormal entity.

Even the practitioners of quantum mechanics finally have agreed that our knowledge, even of the inanimate elements of the world, cannot provide a complete picture. Nature operates in ways not fully deterministic, always tantalizing the observer with the suspicion that something is missing. The most we can predict about any physical system is the probability of its evolving in a variety of ways, but never in the determining view can we predict the evolution of a system in time. The uncertainty principle has reduced the possibility of knowing all of the universe to little more than an educated guess.

What an astrological chart can predict at one level, however, can be altered by man's moral actions, as is stated in the Zohar and previously in my discussions with Velikovsky. Through astrology, we literally will see the moral accountability of man for his actions reflected by the movement of the stars themselves. The following Zohar, emphasizing again that while the stars impel, they do not compel, illustrates the point:

"Over all the stars and constellations of the firmament there have been set chiefs, leaders and ministers whose duty is to serve the world, each one according to his appointed station. And even the tiniest blade of grass on earth has its own appointed star in heaven. Each star, too, has over it a being appointed who ministers before the Lord as its representative, each according to its order. Each and every single star in the firmaments keep vigil over this world. They are appointed to minister to every single object in this world, for to each star there is a peculiar and particular object."[89]

As bizarre and incredible as this Zoharic interpretation of the existence of the stars may sound to the scientific community, a clear purpose associated with celestial bodies nevertheless is provided by the preceding declaration. To the author of the Zohar, the central issue is not the examination of a massive star nearing the end of its life to form a Black Hole. The question addressed by the Kabbalah in general and the Zohar in particular is how and why did it all begin? The Kabbalist declares that stars provide such an inexhaustible supply of energy that they can sustain even so small a physical entity as a blade of grass. Celestial bodies are the mechanism by which metaphysical, primordial energy, which is the totality of an intelligence, becomes manifest. What, then, can be stated with regard to the state of our cosmology that preceded the appearance and manifestation of the galaxies? From what the Zohar has declared, it is clear that the pre-galactic period consisted of unmanifested, infinite numbers of intelligences that became the metaphysical seeds for future manifestation and evolvement. It is the sphere of the absolute where opposing extremes of energy force intelligences merge and become reconciled.

Is this concept any different than that attributed and proven in laboratory tests to DNA? It, too, is the repository of enormous, almost infinite, variations of future manifestations crammed into a volume so minute that it can be seen only through a powerful microscope. From uncountable seeds of uncountable galaxies to infinite seeds of infinite DNA manifestation, the great Zoharic truth once again is demonstrated: "As above, so below."[90] We may paraphrase it to say, "As in the physical universe, so in the metaphysical."

In the metaphysical universe, stars do not shine constantly, transferring energy without cessation. Rather, they are radiant only at appointed intervals. The Zohar continues: "Each unit of consciousness or intelligence returns to its pre-black hole position after having served its purpose."[91]

Thus, our mundane universe and our own physical bodies both reflect and point to a constant back and forth movement between basic reality and the reality of upper, celestial systems which constitute the timeless, spaceless realm we must reach if we are to be true masters of our own destiny. To illustrate the point further, let us reflect for a moment on the response of an atom to outside stimulation. Some of the electrons, when stimulated, become excited and respond by moving into a higher orbit, farther away from the nucleus. Remove the stimulation and they will drop back into their former orbital shells. Infinite changes and emissions of various types of energies almost certainly take place in the process. The same process occurs in our physical bodies on another level. Physical or emotional stimulation of our bodies or psyches elicits different responses, some subtle, some more apparent. Penetration and observation of deeper, more microscopic, areas ultimately will let us see the rapid back and forth movements that take place in this process. Metaphysically some of these movements will even exceed the speed of light at higher orbital levels where the internal intelligences of all DNA are revealed.

Unfortunately, for the present at least, there is no way of knowing whether this rapid movement beyond the speed of light actually exists since we have no instruments capable of detecting or measuring it, but the activity, postulated on the metaphysical plane, very well might be the underlying cause of psychic disorders that constantly baffle our psychiatrists. What seems to emerge from the Zohar is the matter-of-fact declaration that when stimulation is removed from celestial entities, they react precisely in the fashion of entities on the mundane plane by retiring to their former positions. They go back in time, negating Einstein's limiting concept of lightspeed as an absolute, to await the next stimulation, or purpose, that will assign them a functional, manifested program within the total cosmic design. This process, involving entities which truly are intelligences, varies in no way form the internal, pre-programmed function of DNA.

Thus, "far-out" proposals about the universe as described in the Kabbalah become socially acceptable. After all, how and where did this highly intelligent double helix called DNA originate. It is a highly sophisticated programmed computer that defies the imagination of any computer scientist and it must be considered highly likely that after the transition period called death, the higher intelligence forms, of which DNA is only one, continue their existence on levels above the physical. Who can deny that intelligent energy forces go back in time to their former positions, just as electrons do when stimulus is removed. Does it not follow, therefore, that they will return again to the physical plane when proper stimulus — in this case, rebirth through reincarnation — when proper stimulus is resumed?

What, then, are these intelligences that occupy both physical and metaphysical worlds and are capable of moving back and forth between them? Simply stated, they are the direct result of the desire to receive which is the root of all forms of intelligence. When describing the evolution of matter, we really are discussing the evolution of consciousness of the desire to receive. This desire is, in itself, a form of intelligence which is little more than a synonym for consciousness and it consists of four primary aspects of reality[92] in unmanifested form which, in the absolute, had its origin within the Endless. When stimulated with purpose, these four intelligences become the basis of all subsequent manifested physical matter which, in turn, ultimately becomes some life form entity of manifest energy. All the infinite forms of intelligences that crowd our galaxy and others have their origins within the Endless and account for every life form we can observe.

Isaac Luria states[93], "There are four basic realities of intelligence or thought in our mundane universe, namely the inanimate reality, vegetation reality, animal reality and the human reality. These four realities are extensions of the four basic elements of fire, air, water and earth. these four elements are in turn an extended manifestation of the four primal, basic intelligences of the desire to receive, known as the four stimulations of Hesed (Mercy), Gevurah (Judgement), Tiferet (Beauty) and Malkut (Kingdom)."

What is the fundamental character difference between these four realities? Let us begin our investigation with the lowest reality, the inanimate. Why does Luria consider the inanimate kingdom the lowest reality? Ever since mankind entered the new age of subatomic physics, we have begun to understand the enormous activity that takes place within a rock. This energy, contained by all matter, is, according to Luria, an extension and manifestation of one of the aspects of intelligence (stimulus) of the desire to receive. As we penetrate into the reality of matter, we find the smallest, weakest amount of power, desire, stimulation and intelligence of the four realities. A rock does not have the ability either to bring near that which benefits it or to push away that which is harmful. Thus, its level of intelligence and consciousness is the least of all realities.

The desire, or intelligence, of the vegetative species, while similar in this respect to animal and human reality, still does not possess an individuality of consciousness. Its power of desire to reject that which is harmful and to accept that which is beneficial is common to every species of the plant kingdom, but that intelligence stimulates and makes manifest a physical expression of immobility. It cannot, by and within itself, possess the mobility inherent in human and animal realities, yet plants, unlike rocks, do react physically to the stimuli of sunlight, water, heat and cold.

The animal reality is on a higher level of consciousness. Its desire to receive is more intense and its stimulation, or internal energy force, possesses its own individual sense of selection in rejection or acceptance of that which either is harmful or beneficial. Its internal intensity provides for the broader freedom of movement in three dimensions. The freedom of movement seen in the animal kingdom is a direct result of the internal consciousness level already included within its DNA complex. The level of the desire to receive, implanted within the DNA of the plant kingdom, is the primal cause for the manner in which its physical manifestation evolved. Plants do not walk or talk or move in three dimensions because its level of consciousness is of a lower intensity.

The supreme and most intensified desire to receive belongs to the human reality. We are humans simply because the primal cause of activity and the higher levels of conscoiusness include the power to reason and to articulate speech — a gift enjoyed by no other species on earth. Once manifested, it produced a DNA that permitted the physical expression and evolvement of intensified activity. The human reality is not limited by space or time. This intelligent life form has the ability to think about any other reality wherever they may be in our universe. The higher level of consciousness permits man even to think about those who have died generations ago and of those yet unborn to the future. This reality indicates a mobility of the psyche as well as of the body. Thus the concept of expanded consciousness belongs exclusively in the realm of the human reality which relates to and can initiate the interpenetration of the DNA by the level of its desire to receive. Our physical bodies are the ultimate manifestation, end products and result of these higher intelligences that originated within the Endless. Inasmuch as the human reality is not limited by space or time, we *Homo sapiens* have the capability of travel back into time, faster than the speed of light. the Zohar already has declared that within man one can find the exact system that exists in the celestial realm. We may experience the more subtle levels of people and objects, including the interrelationships between people as energy transfers interact between them. In this state, the structure of cosmos opens up to us and shows us its past, present and future, all in one instant that springs free of the space-time continuum.

What seems to emerge from all this is the direct relationship that exists between the four realities and their constant interaction on the most subtle levels. Most important is man's connection and interplay with the cosmic presence. When the Kabbalist speaks with such assurance and delivers his crystal clear interpretation of the cosmic world, he speaks with authority because he has travelled this faster than the lightspeed route. He has returned to and observed the primal state from whence all cosmic presence evolved. By this means, instant communication is possible all across our galaxy and to others as well.

The four realities must be understood if the Kabbalistic method of examination is to be understood. Without that understanding, the Kabbalistic rejection of the common concept that the stars shine at all times, but only reveal themselves to us at night would seem to border upon madness. The Kabbalist, however, knows that things do not happen merely on the physical level. They are directed by an internal energy force of intelligence which interpenetrates particular celestial bodies and evolves into that which we observe in manifest form. The findings of astronomy, confined to the physical realm, have little bearing on the matter.

The human reality transcending the frame of space/time may be seen in the following Zohar: "Come and see if you might think that Moses had no knowledge that he was not to enter the Land of Israel, this is not so. And he therefore preferred knowing about the land prior to his death. Since he wanted to know of it before he departed, he sent spies. When thy failed to bring him back a proper report, he did not send again, but waited until the Lord showed him the land. As it is written, 'Go up unto this mountain, unto Mount Nebo, which is the land of Moab, that is over against Jericho, and behold the land of Canaan which I give unto the Children of Israel for a possession.'[94] And not only viewing the entire land,[95] (which was only possible by the expanding consciousness of Moses, therby permitting him to see the entire breadth and length of Israel from this one vantage point) but in addition, he was shown all future leaders of each generation to come."[96] The relationship between theory and observation is understandably complex. Without observations, theory can only suggest the possibilities, and the uncertainty in prediction of knowledge is something very certain.

Theory, observation and scientific method provide the framework for conceiving and understanding that which has been observed. Observation by itself does not provide the facts required for understanding. When astronomers found new stars and gave them names, only the astrophysicist could associate the incoming energy forces and radiation with these celestial bodies. Actual experience in science, however, seems to add a great deal more confusion to what really is going on than scientific definitions are able to clarify. More often than not, the assumptions and conclusions of science lead into a blind alley. Science is a human undertaking by dedicated humans who, for all their advanced techniques, are subject to mistakes.

The major shortcoming in the area of cosmology lies in the distance that separates man from his cosmos. The untouchables continue to elude the posse of scientists so bent on their capture. Despite the power of the human mind to perceive, sort out and choose from the wealth of information and data provided by space exploration, the mysterious world of outer space continues its flight to the unknown. There can be no marriage between earthlings and the vivid intelligences out there. Their space secrets represent an eternal veil drawn across the universe, cloaking it in utmost secrecy and giving rise to the words of the psalmist. "The heavens declare the glory of the Creator, the expanse of the sky tells of his handiwork."[97] The heavens by no means have yielded up all their mysteries and even as new technological systems are developed, the universe will meet them with new challenges within the frontiers of science.

The Zohar transcends science and when such a comprehensive work appears in the Age of Aquarius, much speculation on the origin of the planets, their cosmic intelligence and their specific purpose in the scheme of things finally will be laid to rest. The Zohar raises questions we never dared to ask, and to receive answers to them, one must go to the Zohar. Let us examine some of the phenomena it presents:

Do stars shine all day long, even though, when bathed in sunlight, we cannot see them. The scientist will assure us that they do, but the Zohar says they do not. Herbs, trees and plants cannot grow and flourish save under the influence of the stars which watch over them from above and gaze upon them face to face, each according to its own particular astral influence.

"Most planets, stars and constellations appear at the beginning of each evening. They usually remain for three hours, less a quarter. From that period on, stars with lesser astral influences appear. However, these stars do not shine or influence in vain. There are those that are conducting and influencing and exercising their own peculiar magnetic fields the entire night so as to enable flowers and plants to grow and blossom.

Then there are those planetary bodies that serve until midnight strikes, performing their particular duties and transferring their own particular magnetic fields until the appointed hour that they have been ministered to share. There are planetary entities that serve the universe for a very short period in the evening. They appear only so long as the blade of grass takes to receive its total sustenance. There is then no further need for these entities to continue ministering their cosmic energies. But no planetary entity stands in vain. As soon as they have finished, have completed their cosmic endeavor, they appear no longer in this world and they return to their appointed place."

"In the book of the higher wisdom of the east," continues the Zohar, "we learn also about the peculiar and particular planetary bodies called a comet. It is a particular star which forms a tail, a scepter, in the firmament. There are certain herbs in our universe, the kind called 'elixirs of life,' that receive their cosmic influence and energy from them. In addition, their cosmic magnetic fields transfer this energy and produce precious stones and fine gold, which forms within the breast of high mountains under shallow water, which are ruled by this particular comet by whose influence they grow and increase. Their cosmic energy is provided by a mere glance at the luminous tail that trails after these comets across the sky that causes those things to flourish.

Certain illnesses of man, as jaundice, can be cured through the patient's gazing upon shining steel which is held before his eyes, and rapidly moved from side to side, so that, like a comet's tail, it sends flashes of light into the face, thus healing the disease. Therefore all those objects over which such stars as these are appointed can have no proper development and growth unless the light of the comet actually passes over them. They are then enabled to renew their color and their energy according to their need. It is similarly indicated in the Book of King Solomon, in regard to the science of precious stones, that when these stones are denied the light and sparkle of certain stars, their development is retarded and they never reach their full perfection. The Lord has ordered all things so that the world may be perfected and beautified. Accordingly, it is written that the stars are 'to give light upon earth in all the things which the world needs for its perfection."[98]

I can't say for certain that the cosmic traveller referred to in the Zohar is Halley's comet. What seems to emerge from the Zohar's explanation of the comet Sharvit is more than merely some sort of celestial spectacle. Comets fundamentally are cosmic energy capsules. The shining tail that produces a beautiful evening star streaming halfway across the sky therefore is more than merely a sight to observe.

6

What's In a Name?

"What's in a name? A rose, by any other name would smell as sweet...."

—William Shakespeare, *Romeo and Juliet*

ILLIAM SHAKESPEARE WROTE SOME BEAUTIFUL POETRY, BUT had he been a student of Kabbalah he would have come up with a different answer to Romeo's plaintive question. What's in a name? Everything is in a name. It is the lynchpin of control; the dividing line between blind destiny and free will. Witness Adam's first assigned task in the Garden of Eden:[99]

"And out of the ground the Lord God formed every beast of the field, and every fowl of the air; and brought them unto Adam to see what he would call them: and whatsoever Adam called every living creature, that was the name thereof."

The exercise was designed to do far more than keep Adam occupied and insulate him from ennui. Of all the fears that bedevil mankind, none is so terrifying as fear of the unknown because what is unknown can neither be avoided nor controlled. Which warning would you rather hear whispered on a dark night: "A tiger is out there" or "Something is out there"? Which strikes the greater chill?

By naming the creatures of a newly formed world, Adam became the master of his environment, but he was not the last of his line to wield the power of a name. Generations later, guided by the hand of the Lord, a man named Abram was to refine the art in a fashion calculated to change the history of the world.

Again from Genesis: "Now the lord said unto Abram, set thee out of thy country and from thy kindred and from thy father's house unto the land that I will show thee. And I will make thee a great nation and I will bless thee and make thy name great and be thou a blessing. I will bless them that bless thee and him that curseth thee I will curse. In thee shall all the families of the earth be blessed." And, the text continues, "And the Lord appeared unto Abram and said 'unto thy seed I will give this land.'"

The promise was a heady one, but Abram, who was wise in the ways of the Chaldeans and an adept in the science of astrology, had reason for skepticism. His wife, Sarai, was barren. Abram had no seed to receive the land offered and he saw in the stars, as if carved in stone, that he was destined to die childless, leaving all his worldly goods to distant relatives.

And Abram said "Oh Lord! What will Thou giveth me since I go forth hence childless and he that shall be possessor of my house is Eliezer of Damascus? Behold, to me Thou has given no seed and, lo, one born in my house is to be mine heir." And, behold, the word of the Lord came unto him saying: "This man shall not be thine heir, but he that shall come forth out of thine own bowels shall be thine heir."[101]

Then, in a process that would turn the skeptic into a man of such faith that he later would prepare, without question, to sacrifice his only son at a holy command, The Lord revealed to Abram the metaphysical mechanism by which he might rewrite the destiny he saw in the stars. Abram, at the command of the Lord, would add the Hebrew letter hay to his name, changing it to Abraham, and his wife, Sarai, would become Sarah. By this process, they seized the reins of destiny and changed their stars in an act of free will.

And the Lord brought him (Abram) outside and said: 'Look now toward heaven and count the stars, if thou be able to count them.' And He said unto him "So shall thy seed be. And he believed in the Lord and He counted it to him for righteousness.'"

As with everthing in the coded text of the Bible, the central message is packaged with several others and before we delve into metamechanics of the horoscope — altering name change, it may be well to examine a few of them. The dialogue between the Lord and Abram would seem to indicate a normal conversation between two individuals — almost as if both were conversing in Abram's home. After making the promise, ". . . he that comes forth out of thine own bowels shall be thy heir," the Lord takes Abram "outside." What, however, is "outside" or "inside" to the Lord. As the Creator, he is all pervading and omnipresent; the all-inclusive Positive Energy discussed in detail in "Kabbalah for the Layman."[102] The shift, from that metaphysical reality to the metaphor of the physical plane, introduced the anthropomorphic God upon which all great religions since have been based.

The impersonal Lord, a pure Energy devoid of physical form or substance, is one with which few people can connect or feel affinity, but when, in this dialogue with Abram, the Creator was cast in something approaching human form, it became incumbent upon all subsequent believers to recognize His presence as all pervading, whether or not they understood the Kabbalistic maxim that that which is to be revealed first must be concealed. The concealment of total spirit in an anthropomorphic image in order to reveal it to mankind was the factor designed eventually to end war, hatred, greed and envy. The fact that such a blissful state of harmony never materialized certainly does no credit to existing religions.

Still, when the word "Lord" appears in the Bible as a personal, intimate concept, the possibility of our connecting and creating an affinity with the Creator has become enormously enhanced. Thus, when the Kabbalistic decodification of the word "Lord" indicates an all-pervading intelligent force, present in everything in and around us, connection becomes self-realized with one's personal makeup and psyche eternally bound up and connected with it. It then is only logical to decide that one had best learn what this intelligent force is all about, what makes it tick and, more importantly, to become very careful not to behave in a way in which the energy flow process may be disturbed. In short, if stealing, hating, envying and making war are obstacles to being a functional creature, then second thoughts should be given to any temptation to embark upon a course of negativity. Crime, in the long run, really does not pay. The perceived liabilities vastly outweigh the short-term gain.

Seen in that light, no human soul would be so foolish as to antagonize this internal, intelligent force or invite its wrath. No one can fool an intelligence. Our own internal energy, not some outside force, is at stake, and that internal energy is very important because it is the force that permits growth and movement without which the individual is dead. That resolved, let us return to the vital dialogue between Abram and a suddenly corporeal Lord. What does His request that Abram go outside and count the stars mean and what is its connection with the preceding verse saying, "This man shall not be thine heir, but he that has come forth out of thine own bowels shall be thine heir?" Was it necessary for the Lord to prove his point by telling Abram to count the stars, or was the order given to shore up Abram's wavering faith?

In another verse, Abram "believed in the Lord and He counted it to him as righteousness,"[101] but is Abram really to be commended for believing, after having been told that just as he cannot count the stars, so shall be his seed? Believing is not a concept in the lexicon of Kabbalah. When one says, "I believe," he instantly declares his disbelief. Only when he says, "I know," does he erase all doubt. But Abram had to be made to understand that he must grasp a higher level of consciousness if he was to accept the Lord's bounty. He could not remain in the lower, parallel state where a son could not be born. He would have to leave the lower level where he was known in the stars as Abram and rise to the level of Koh where he would be known as Abraham in a metaphysical realm into which the internal cosmic influences of celestial bodies pervade. Koh indicates the holy name which was linked to him on the side of higher levels of consciousness. It is the gateway of prayer through which man obtains his requests.

When the Creator added the letter hay both to the names of Abram and Sarai, saying 'Neither shall thy name any more be called Abram but you shall be Abraham, for the father of a multitude of nations have I made thee,"[102] He actually was creating an acronym from two abbreviations, Av and Hamon, which literally means "father of a multitude of nations". The previous name, Abram, meant simply father of Aram which is the place from which he came. The Lord then told Abraham to cast new horoscopes and prepare new natal charts for himself and his wife, using the name changes as a new moment of birth. Abraham therefore was raised to a new level of consciousness and given an entirely new set of planetary influences, altering the previous destiny that said he never would father a child. It was that act that gave rise to the tradition that Israel is not governed by the stars.

We now can comprehend the importance of the different levels of consciousness that one can achieve and use literally to alter one's destiny. Man does, in effect, create his own destiny and neither that fact nor the astrological natal chart are in conflict. The chart of a destiny may be predicted, but because the stars impel, but do not compel, it also can be changed.

To this day, an old Orthodox Jewish tradition is to change the name of a person who is gravely ill with an eye toward changing his destiny of death. This still is done by the Research Centre for Kabbalah in Israel when we conduct retreats. We concentrate upon particular names and changes of names because names are much more than labels by which we introduce ourselves to people. From a Kabbalistic point of view, a Biblical name relates to the metaphysical, non-limiting aspect of space and time and becomes a channel for metaphysical transfers of energy. Thus, when a person is ill, we gather many people together for concentration and a drawing down by the meditative process of energy to their benefit. Strange as the practice may seem in this technological age, many people will testify that the rebirth accompanying a name change, and the new natal chart that results, has healed them.

It is well established that the changing of a name elevates the individual to a higher level of consciousness. Christian clerics of the Roman Catholic persuasion have followed the practice for years, frequently taking a Biblical name or a name sacred to their doctrine upon entering holy orders. This does not mean, however that all one has to do is proclaim a new name for himself or get the civil courts to proclaim one for him. There is no spiritual validity to the court process and before any name change can have the desired effect, the individual first must strive to change his own desire to receive for the self alone to a desire to receive for the sake of sharing.

Whatever the process required and whatever the method instituted, however, the Zohar gives clear indication of the validity of astrology and the absolute influence that celestial bodies manifest upon the universe, and, more importantly, that we can change the destinies that have been programmed for us. Abraham changed his name and removed himself from his own natal astrological influences, but he did more than that. He changed his address as well. Remember, in Gen., "The Lord said unto Abram, set thee out of thy country and from thy kindred and from thy father's house unto the land that I will show thee . . ." What seems to be indicated by rabbinical sources, the Zohar included, is the expression "Mi shane Makom, Me shane Mazel" which means that when one changes the place in which he lives, he also will induce a metaphysical change in his personal constellation. All of us come into life facing things we cannot control, yet life does seem to be a curious amalgam of inexorable fate and free will. Contrary to the highest precept of democracy, all men are not created equal. Through reincarnation and the tikune process, they are created with a multitude of handicaps, burdens and travails, and overcoming these is another process entirely.

As dealt with in detail in "Kabbalah for the Layman,"[104] the universe began under the law of cause and effect which, of course, corresponds with the Biblical verse, "Whatever a man soweth, that shall he also reap; they that plow iniquity and sow wickedness reap the same."[105] That translates directly to the metaphysical law of tikune which is parallel to the physical Newtonian law that states, "for every action there is an equal, opposite reaction." The only difference between the universal law of tikune and the physical law observed at the mundane level is the scope which each one actually embraces.

With the advent of Einsteinian physics came a clue as to how we can reconcile both aspects of the same universal whole. Cause and effect on one level will produce everything according to the universal law of cause and effect. Other elements, however, can alter the entire existence and composition of the very same thing.

Astrology is a science that provides us with predictable information coinciding with the aspect of fate along the lines of Newtonian classical physics. When we consider the aspect of achieving another level of consciousness, we are not rejecting science. We are merely taking in the broader spectrum of things extant at the more subtle, subatomic level to alter the same universal law of cause and effect. Each must be applied on a different level. The law of tikune is a continuous experience because so long as tikune is not achieved as the result of a life stipulated by prior incarnations, we can safely state that the universal law of cause and effect has come into play and there is little one can do to alter it at that level.

Once one has ascended the spiritual ladder which is the key to achieving tikune and correcting the faults and flaws of prior incarnations, he then has altered the state of the flaw and with it, that parallel level of consciousness that dictates the path he will take throughout his lifetime. The achievement permits him to elevate to another level of consciousness by the process of tikune. Such an individual has, in fact, repaired the original flaw that brought the expected metaphysical DNA pattern in his life. Thus, what we are considering when discussing parallel levels, or altered states of consciousness, is a literal move from one metaphysical DNA level pattern to another.

It is not my intent at this point to present a real case for the authenticity or validity of reincarnation. That ground already has been covered in "Wheels of a Soul." The point is made here simply to emphasize that knowledge of astrology enables the individual to provide a rational explanation of life and its mysteries based on the ascertainable law of cause and effect. The metaphysical DNA is merely a printout of the individual's previous lifetimes. Based on his past behavior, the infinite actions, both positive and negative, a new, reborn, metaphysical DNA is created as the embodiment of all these prior actions. The interface between the physical and metaphysical realm, between the present and composite metaphysical DNA, is the lineup of the astral bodies at the time of his birth.

The Kabbalistic view of astrology, however, is dramatically different from the conventional pursuit of the science. Conventional astrology contends that the individual will take a course of action because of the arrangement of the stars, whereas Kabbalah contends the tikune process puts the individual in an astrological position so that the stars will impel him in the needed direction. Are birth charts a pictorial view of the metaphysical interface or merely the result of a physically expressed view of a predictable future? The Kabbalistic answer will affirm that physical entities in no way determine or affect the prior metaphysical realm. It is rather this unknowable, non-material, realm that contains the determining internal cosmic energy force that ultimately will make manifest the particular channels of energy by which the space-time energy field becomes a reality. The planets simply represent the life-giving forces, the internal or external stimulation in any given area of life.

In astronomy-astrology, we are dealing with combinations of complex life forces and expressions that subsequently become manifest in our physical plane. The process may be compared to the seed of the male which contains the total complex of life forces, along with the peculiar channels of energy by which these same internal energy forces subsequently become manifest. It is for this reason that the positioning of the complex mechanism of planetary bodies, present at the time of birth, act as a physical interface for the metaphysical interface that encompasses the complete printout of prior lifetimes. In short, the stars determine nothing. They do not compel. They merely impel.

The basic destiny pattern is considered fundamentally unalterable. Therefore, when we have a sequence of experiences which the natal chart almost could predict with 100 percent accuracy, we see an individual dealing with his own incarnation, which is the reason why he was born at a particular time in a particular country to be under the particular astral influences of that given moment. Consequently, when we read in the Zohar that these astral influences dictate to the enormous and profound extent that they do, it is a result of the reincarnation process, which in effect, was the result of prior flaws in a prior lifetime. From an astrological point of view, the exact time and place of birth does, in effect, reveal the individual's primary — and I stress *primary* — life pattern: His potential, power, attachments and his problems. What the chart is revealing is merely an insight into the pattern of prior incarnations.

For all the inviolability of the basic destiny pattern, however, we have a degree of freedom almost without limitation to determine how the tikune process will be created in the present lifetime. The natal chart reveals the blinders and restrictions that will keep us from feeling free so that we ultimately can make use of the tools that are available by which we can transcend to another level of consciousness. Those blinders are of our own manufacture. We built them in prior lifetimes, but because we created them, we can break them and ascend to a higher level of consciousness.

This higher level of consciousness obviously will come about through a higher form of meditation and by not only having, but by living an ideal, spiritual way of life. Then and then only can we truly be liberated from the pattern of destiny that seems so unalterable and come to grips with our problems. Then we can ascend and alter the initial natal chart.

A commitment to self-knowledge and self-improvement is the first requirement of any individual who wishes to take control of his life and alter his destiny, but once that commitment is made, the results can be immediate and fulfilling. Not only will he be happier in the quest to elevate his soul, but he will find that pursuit of the goal begins to alleviate a great deal of the suffering initially dictated by his tikune pattern. Suddenly, he will notice that much of the confusion and discouragement that seemed so overwhelming gradually is beginning to disappear. This phenomenon is not necessarily the result of altering the natal chart, which is the ultimate goal; it will come about simply because his commitment will result in the improvement and quality of his lifestyle, an alteration without which no one can reach the higher level of consciousness necessary to secure a new chart and thus achieve rebirth.

Anyone recognizable today as a truly spiritual person has paid this price. Because of the universal tikune pattern, it is safe to say that he was not born to such elevation. It was only through self development that he ultimately changed the pattern of his life and achieved another level of consciousness. Rabbi Hiam Vital, the exclusive student of Rabbi Isaac Luria, actually received something in the area of one hundred different souls in the course of his lifetime, each of which represented a different level of consciousness. Such power is available to anyone who diligently seeks it, but, as with all things worth having, it is not free and guidance toward the goal often is wanting.

The best of astrologers can err in the effort to accurately chart an individual's course. He may find flaws or discrepancies in the chart's predictions, but they are of little use unless further investigation is made into the lifestyle of the individual seeking advice. More often than not, the individual will provide information that will indicate ascension to another level of consciousness that can completely throw off the predictions of any natal chart. This is the common weakness of the conventional astrologer who neither considers an alteration of the chart possible nor seeks to plumb the present life of his client.

In the interpretation of any chart, almost any factor can be regarded as an implication of tikune, but it will not appear to the practitioner who fails to consider the point, because search as he may within his conventional framework, he will not detect subtle shifts in the level of consciousness. Such perceptions do not come from the chart. They come from the intuition of the individual astrologer who truly is looking for a synthesis between the planets and the chart and direct impressions of the living person. One of the constructive uses of astrology necessitates knowledge not only of what astrology can do for us, but of its limitations as well. The individual's level of consciousness cannot be based purely upon astrological data or upon the seeker's intelligence and acquired knowledge. It must be based upon the individual's spiritual lifestyle.

Our present lifetime comprises the sum total of all previous lifetimes and only with comprehension of all previous experience can one find in his chart a composite of what he really has been. All that we have been, both good and bad, is contained in the present life chart. Once the faults have been found, either through a competent astrological reading or through rigorous self-examination, the individual will be able to pinpoint the negative aspect of prior lifetimes and, by growing spiritually, change the patterns that have been consistent to alter astral predictions and change his destiny.

Skeptics who brand astrology as a parlor game at best and a cynical con game at worst, long have asked how the position of the planets at the time of a person's birth possibly can have any bearing upon their subsequent lives. They have not only the right, but the responsibility, to ask that question. Just as the most important question a Kabbalist can ask is "Why?" the most important obligation of the Kabbalist is to answer that question, and, with regard to planetary influences, that is what we shall attempt to do at this point.

Planetary and astral influences are nothing more than bodies of energy, both negative and positive. A person is born at a particular time so that when his soul enters its corporeal body it will absorb the combination of energies dictated by the cargo of tikune carried from past lives. As the soul travels through the metaphysical space between the endless and mundane worlds, it passes through various levels of energies, picking up what is required both of good and bad influences in terms of habits and attitudes carried over from the totality of its previous incarnations. The planets thus are symbols of more than merely physical dimensions. Their placement, at the moment of birth, can be compared to a program entered into a computer, except that this computer is as massive as the billions of stars and planets of which it is constructed. What emerges is the "software" of the individual's present life with the good and the evil, the strength and the weakness, of previous lives neatly formatted from the eternal computer's memory bank. The importance of placement of the planetary and astral bodies for that purpose is no less than the importance of all the binary bits of information necessary to construct the program sought for a terrestrial computer.

The natal chart, therefore, provides us with what amounts to a movie of our prior incarnations. Every action of sin and sanctification is stamped there at and by the moment of birth. The moment of birth, therefore, is not a random event. Whether it occurs prematurely or extends to the phenomenon of "the 10-month baby," it is specifically designed to assure that the individual arrives in this life with every bit of the baggage he accumulated in the last one. The soul without baggage obviously would have no reason to return.

When an individual is born on a particular day, at a particular time, in a particular place, the Kabbalistic astrologer is given an easily read blueprint of that person's psyche and with it, knowledge of how the individual may be able to alter the in-born program and create another whereby he may escape the chains of predestination. It is precisely in this area of free will that this book will differ from other books on astrology. Many of them contend there is no exercise of free will. The Kabbalist knows that we may or may not shun our responsibilities and therefore may or may not live up to our true possibilities. Therefore, free will is unlimited.

The natal chart need not be on a collision course with free will. The man who relaxes before reaching his limit is an unhappy failure. The one who explores the limits of his capacities will be a success, but both will exist within the limited framework of this universe. It is precisely in this area that the science of astrology has not met its responsibility which is to provide a palatable answer to the apparent contradiction between fate and free will.

If the contradiction never has been successfully met by conventional astrology, however, the parallel aspect certainly has. Witness this story from the Zohar:[106]

"Rabbi Jose and Rabbi Haia were traveling together and they saw in front of them two other men going along. They saw a third man come up to them and say, 'I beg of you, give me some food, if only a piece of bread, because for two days I have been wandering in this forest without tasting anything. I am lost.' One of the two men thereupon took out the food which he had brought with him for the journey through the forest and gave him to eat and drink. Said his companion to him, 'What will you do for food? For I am going to eat my own. As you know, we both have taken sufficient food to last us the several days' journey through the forest and if I were to share my bread and drink with you, then both of us will perish.' Whereupon his friend replied, 'Do I want to eat yours?' The poor man ate up all that he received except a small morsel of bread and the individual in turn gave him even this last piece of bread for the road. Whereupon Rabbi

Jose felt that possibly they should share with this individual who had completely given of his to this poor man upon which Rabbi Haia remarked, 'The Lord does not desire that we interfere at this point with his tikune process. And then Rabbi Haia added, 'Perhaps that man was doomed to some punishment and the Lord sent this man to him so as to deliver him.'

The two resumed their journey with Rabbi Haia and Rabbi Jose following at a distance so as not to be noticed. And shortly thereafter, the man who had given his food away became faint. Said his companion to him, 'Did I not tell you not to give your bread away?' Rabbi Jose then said to Rabbi Haia, 'We have bread. Let's give him some.' To which replied Rabbi Jose, 'Do you want to undo the merit of this good deed? Let us watch closely, for surely the pallor of death is on this man's face and the Lord prepared some merit for him in order to deliver him.'

Meanwhile, the man fell asleep under a tree and his companion left him to carry on as he had told him before. Then Rabbi Jose and Rabbi Haia saw a fiery adder by him. 'Alas for that man,' said Rabbi Haia. 'Surely he will now be killed.' Rabbi Jose replied, 'He deserves that a miracle should be done on his behalf.'

At that point, a snake came down from the tree with intent to kill the man, but the adder attacked and killed it, then turned its head and departed. Said Rabbi Jose, 'Did I not tell you that the Lord desired to perform a miracle for him and that you should not exhaust his merit?' For what had been forcasted in the stars, that this man was doomed to some form of punishment, his merit stood up for him.

The man then woke up and began to go. Rabbi Haia and Rabbi Jose came up to him and gave him food. When he had eaten, they then told him of the miracle which the Lord had performed for him. Rabbi Jose then quoted the verse, 'Trust in the Lord and do good. Dwell in the land and follow after faithfulness.'[107]

The Zohar then explains, "Happy is the man who does good with what he has because he arouseth good for the entire universe with righteousness. Because righteousness is the Tree of Life and it arouseth itself against the tree of Death and takes those who are attached to it and delivers them from death. "As it is written, "Charity delivers one from death."[108] And what roused it to do so you must say the charity that man does. As it were, he performs it above also.

What emerges, yet again, from this beautiful Zohar is the fact that while the stars impel, they do not compel. The natal chart of the man in question, because of prior incarnations, led him into the wilderness with the opportunity to change his destiny. There is no question that an astrologer, reading his chart, would have come up with the prediction of his death. A good astrologer, however, knows there is certain information he must not share. He must never predict anyone's death, no matter how evident it may appear in the natal chart, lest he create a self-fulfilling prophecy negating that possible altered state of consciousness that would have changed the grim destiny.

The man in the forest had seized the opportunity offered in a single moment to reach another level of consciousness. He offered to sacrifice his own life for the benefit of another. His companion held that action to be foolhardy, but the Zohar demonstrates that the life of the individual—definitely was forfeit. He was going to die. It was assured, until at the given moment of opportunity, he exercised his free will to obey the commandment, "Love thy neighbor,"[109] and at that moment, his fate was altered in a fashion the best of astrologers never could have foretold.

Another illustration that the stars impel, but do not compel, is classically illustrated by the most illustrious sage of all time, Rabbi Akiva Ben Joseph, already mentioned.

For all the sages' use and study of astrology, however, their writings also are filled with warnings against its use in predicting future events. What concerned the Rabbis of that day was the aspect of idol-worship and acceptance of a predicted fate that would have negated the individual's free will. Few today are likely to make false gods of astrological entities, but the danger of fatalism remains. A good astrologer must understand that the natal chart alone does not tell the full story. While the individual is born into certain circumstances about which he has absolutely no say—his parents, his ancestors, his social standing or, for that matter, physical or mental characteristics—he can, as we have discussed at length, take control of his life and change his chart. It must be noted at this point, however, that his parents do have a choice in determining the characteristics of their own children,[110] but certain conditions are present at birth as are the tools with which each of us work out our lives. Many astrologers, taking it no farther than that, err on the side of fatalism.

If astrology draws its share of skeptics, reincarnation, upon which Kabbalistic astrology is based, attracts even more, yet the Bible and the Zohar are full of references that clearly support the premise.

"Then the word of the Lord came to me, saying, 'Before I formed thee in the belly, I knew thee, and before thou camest forth out of the womb, I sanctified thee, and I ordained thee a prophet unto the nations.' "[111]

The verse suggests the idea of repeated existences upon Earth and additionally sets forth the prediction concerning the future of the life of Jeremiah, that he would indeed become a prophet. Does the passage not indicate fate and predictable destiny as opposed to free will? The concept of parallel levels, here too, provides the reader with deeper insight into the dialogue between the Lord and Jeremiah. This revolutionary idea is further strengthened by the following passage in the Zohar:[112]

"Rabbi Abba began a discourse on the verse: 'Counsel in the heart of a man is like deep water; but a man of understanding will draw it out.[113] The first clause of this verse, he said, 'may be applied to the Lord (the internal cosmic energy force) who with deep counsel (the wide array of the complexities of prior incarnations) molded events by the hand of Joseph so as to execute his decree, but a man of understanding will draw it out (make manifest the other, altered states of consciousness).' "

This is exemplified in Joseph who revealed those deeper, more subtle, levels which the Lord decreed in this world. "Counsel in the heart of man is like deep water" is exemplified by Judah at the time when he approached Joseph on behalf of Benjamin, as explained in "The Kabbalah Connection,"[114] whereas "a man of understanding" is exemplified in Joseph. What emerges from the Zohar are the partial levels that accompany man in his universal travel through time. Joseph represents a level of altered states of consciousness that links up with the outer space connection — the intelligence level of Yesod as explained in "The Kabbalah Connection." Joseph is an individual and a man of understanding "who will draw it out." Judah, linked with the intelligence level of Malkhut, is represented by the section of the verse that says "Counsel in the heart of a man is like deep water," which is just another way of saying that one who has great knowledge is of no use to me if he cannot impart it. It is toward the cosmic level of Joseph, which draws one to the more subtle reality of consciousness, that this new dimension of altered states can be reached. This is the central theme of Kabbalistic cosmic consciousness and pure awareness.

Information provides knowledge only if connection is made. The library is full of information, but it remains useless to a man who cannot read, and therefore cannot make it manifest. Some people, on the other hand, are "book smart." They know all the facts and figures by rote, but they cannot apply them. One must achieve an altered state of consciousness and pure awareness to make connection. Joseph knew how. Judah did not.

All of the foregoing may seem complex and abstruse at first glance, but in reality, wholeness and simplicity lie at the soul of the Zohar, a fact made clear by the following passage:

"Rabbi Abba was one day sitting at a gate of Lydda, when he saw a man come and seat himself on a ledge overhanging the ground. Being weary from traveling, he fell asleep. Rabbi Abba suddenly saw a serpent glide up towards the man, but before it reached him, a small serpent known in Aramaic as Custifa Dikuradonna attacked the serpent and killed it. The man then woke up, and catching sight of the serpent in front of him, stood up and walked away from the ledge. And no sooner had he done so than the ledge gave way and crashed into the hollow beneath it.

Rabbi Abba then approached him and said, 'Tell me, what have you done that God should have performed two miracles for you?' To which the man replied, 'Never did anyone do an injury to me, but that I made peace with him and forgave him. Moreover, if I could not make peace with him, I did not retire to rest before I forgave him together with all those who vexed me. Nor was I at any time concerned about evil that the man did to me. Nay, moreover from that day onward, I exerted myself to show kindness to such a man.'"[115]

At this point, one might wonder why the serpent is a recurring theme throughout the Bible and the Zohar. Its imagery is essential because it represents the negative side of man. The Hindu aspect, in which the coiled serpent is the sexual power of kundalini, is regarded as a positive force, but in the Bible, it is always negative. Sex can be both negative and positive as when the desire to have a child alters the state of consciousness and becomes positive, but in the Kabbalistic view, serpent power always is negative power, brought on by man's negative activity. When a thief steals, he creates a serpent that will strike him when he least expects it, proving, in short, that crime does not pay.

The point of the preceding Zohar, however, is to show that transformation of an individual to higher spiritual ideals is possible and that as a result, interpretations of a natal chart may be completely outmoded. Obviously, when one takes this more comprehensive approach, based upon recognition of a reality much higher than that perceived by our physical senses, it becomes evident that the most important indications in a natal chart will not come from the outer world, but from within. The more one consciously is in touch with one's inner self, the more astrology has to offer him. This is not to imply that we thus have a new may of manipulating our fate, but that astrology becomes a means of clarifying for us various stages of self-development in which we ultimately can transform our selves and produce a new natal chart and a new stage of personal existence.

To further demonstrate how the individual literally can alter his chart and make manifest his entire life's destiny, I return once again to the Zohar:[116]

"Such is one as Rabbi Shimon Bar Yohai in whose days the world never required a sign of the rainbow. For whatever punishment was decreed against the world, he could annul it.

One day, he was sitting at the gate of Lydda when he lifted up his eyes and saw the light of the sun darkened three times and black and yellow spots appearing in the sun.

He said to his son, Rabbi Elazar, 'Follow me, my son, and let us see what happens, for of a surety, some punishment is decreed above and the Lord desires to let me know."

Such a decree is kept in suspense 30 days and the Lord does not carry it out before making it known to the righteous. As it is written: 'For the Lord will do nothing but that he reveal his secrets to his servants the prophets.'[117]

They came into a vineyard where they saw a serpent advancing like a curl of fire along the ground. Rabbi Shimon shook his garments and brought his hand down on the head of the serpent, which then came to a halt, though its tongue was still moving. He said to it, 'Serpent, Serpent. Go and tell that Supernal Serpent that Rabbi Shimon is still alive.' It then put its head into a hole in the ground. He said, 'I ordain that just as this serpent has returned to its hole in the ground, so will the supernal one return to the hollow of the greater beast.'

Rabbi Shimon then began to pray, and as they were praying they heard a voice say, 'Ye ministers of evil return to your place. Ye band of ruffians abide not in the world, for Rabbi Shimon Bar Yohai annuls your power. Happy are thou, Rabbi Shimon, that thy master is solicitous for thy honor at all times above that of all other men.'

By this time, he saw that the sun was shining again, and the blackness had passed. He said, 'Surely the world is safe again.' He then went into his house and expounded the verse, 'For the Lord is righteous. He loves righteousness and the upright shall behold his face.'"[118]

The black and yellow spots seen by Rabbi Shimon Bar Yohai today would be known as sun spots—titanic storms on the surface of earth's primary—but from ancient times, their symbolism was one of some great darkness about to befall the world. From the foregoing, we can see that not only can one often change one's own personal life destiny, but the destiny of the world as well, no matter what astrological charts may proclaim. Rabbi Shimon was able to face deadly peril from the serpent and bend it to his will, but the Zohar shows that such capability lies within reach of anyone who truly strives for an elevated level of consciousness. With such power, we not only are capable of controlling our own destiny, but we can have tangible, measurable impact upon the affairs of men as well.

It is absolutely vital that the astrologer inject the essence of these two important Zohars into any aspect of fate prediction vs. free will. Unhappily, most astrologers have no access to this knowledge and many of them virtually become what the sages feared they might become — idol worshippers, giving homage to signs of celestial bodies because they know these bodies do indeed contain the cosmic energies that influence the universe. Knowing only that, however, they are in no position to do anything that could avert impending disaster. Therefore, they worship, hoping that by worship, they can quell the wrath of these so-called gods to bring peace on earth and strength and energy to the universe. Given the wisdom of the Zohar, Rabbi Shimon Bar Yohai was able to take direct action and, harnessing the power of the Creator, turn a preordained catastrophe aside.

Keep in mind that there is nothing metaphysical or mystical about the idea of prediction. The concept, unfortunately, is so shrouded in the mumbo-jumbo of mysticism that we lose sight of the fact that predictions and prophesies, whether they turn out to be right or wrong, are very much a mundane function of our day-to-day lives. Television commentators, using exit polls, surveys and computer extrapolations, forecast every presidential election, often with amazing accuracy, even before the polls have closed in California. Every evening newscast features a weatherman who, by using satellite photos and interpreting isobars, highs and lows, predicts the weather for the next seven days. Such activities obviously fall under the purview of prophecy, though no one would call it that. There is nothing metaphysical about an exit poll. There is nothing mystical about a weather satellite.

Physicians also are prophets in their own right. They analyze, diagnose, and confidently predict the course of any given illness. Their prognostications are based upon education, experience and logic. We certainly would not call a physician a mystic, though there is a certain grim parallel between public reaction to the prophet of the Bible and the physician of today. If the prophet of old turned out to be wrong, he was stoned to death. If the physician is wrong, he is sued for malpractice, but forecasting the future is commonplace even as we move into the 21st century.

Why, then, is the proposition of forcasting the future through in-
formed study of the stars and planets and their interaction with other
celestial bodies a suspect activity? Celestial bodies are harbingers of
things to come simply because they make manifest, at given times,
unique cosmic energies applying to individuals born under their
specific influences. Astrology, the weather, politics all are merely
manifestations of the flow of cosmic energy and just as we can predict
events by means of data programmed into a computer, we can accomplish the same thing, right down to the parameters of the individual soul, by means of the cosmic computer. Through astrology,
the cosmic computer is capable of delivering a better, more intimate
picture of the individual that that of which he, himself, is aware.

If we can evolve such skills, then an opportunity is presented which
should be sought, learned and used at will. In relationships, we frequently are fooled by the appearance of what people seem to be,
simply because all of us put up defenses against the world in which we
live. The drawback to such a necessary survival mechanism is that if
the individual, through his various shields and personas, can fool
others, then quite naturally he also can fool himself. Given the truth
from an astrological standpoint, we can readily know both the
positive and the negative aspects of an individual as well as of
ourselves, and if we can do that, our own lives can become a
bit easier.

As we have learned through Kabbalah, the roots of human conduct
always are mystical. They are concealed from the naked eye and
there is no way of proving anything in the nature of the spirit of man.
By examination of the soul, however, since the soul, as an internal
force, makes manifest the inner nature of man, we can detect the true
motives and aims of those with whom we must deal in this life.
Without the capability of inward probing, provided by astrology and
the Kabbalah, all we can do is observe physical manifestations, and
those seldom will give answers beyond what the individual
manifesting them desires to make public. Through Kabbalah, we can
probe the internal mechanism that makes this complicated machine
called "Man" really work.

I'm not saying that astrology and a natal chart comprise the answer, but astrology, with the Kabbalah, can provide the fundamental tools needed for examination of everything around us. That is why I believe that astrology, as a study of reincarnation, is one of the most important techniques by which the individual can follow his own inner spirit, which usually is concealed even from himself.

Much is made today of solar energy, which is seen as the only alternative to a dwindling supply of natural resources on earth, but modern scientific knowledge of the sun has little edge on what the Zohar already has told us. We are aware of periodic explosive solar flares and sun spots, but so was the Zohar. What else was Rabbi Shimon Bar Yohai discribing in the Zohar quoted earlier? Now, however, scientists have discovered another solar phenomenon called "coronal holes". These are rips in the surface of the sun — that blanket of searing gas called the corona. This blinding shroud usually is uniform in character, but occasionally, it fails to maintain its equilibrium and a coronal hole develops through which awesome gusts of solar wind in the form of charged particles come roaring to disrupt the earth's magnetic field ninety-three million miles away.

The phenomenon still is under study, but if astrology is added to the science of astronomy, one begins to understand what the Zohar means when it says that there is not a single blade of grass that is not influenced in its daily growth by such vast cosmic energy fields. The astronomer also will realize that the activities of man cause this phenomena. Astronomy alone will not explain the full extent of the massive bombardment from cosmos constantly undergone by our planet's atmosphere, but the Zohar stretches the dimensions, illustrating that what is happening on a physical level, ineffectual as it may seem to the man in the street, is occurring with equal force on the metaphysical level, affecting the entire universe through channels transferred to us by planetary and stellar entities. To scorn such knowledge, simply because scientists are uncomfortable with any entity that cannot be put in a test tube for "double blind" laboratory testing, is more than unconscionable. In an increasingly complex world, it is dangerous.

7

Pathways to the Stars

"Certainty in science is good, although impossible. . . . Certainty in religion is bad, although common."
— Phil Donahue, *The Human Animal*

ARISTOTLE, LONG RANKED AS ONE OF THE WISEST OF THE Greeks, contemplated the universe and proclaimed that the Earth was its center, with the Sun, Moon and stars in majestic orbit around it. At the physical level, Aristotle the scientist was wrong.

After first reviling him, however, the Christian church finally decided that he was right and made his paradigm such a rigidly enforced point of religious dogma that centuries had to pass before other scientists, such as Galileo and Copernicus, dared set the record straight. A strange paradox arises from the scenario. Both Aristotle, who could not be certain because he lacked essential data, and religion, which was certain because religion requires no data, were right, not wrong, but neither of them had the remotest clue as to why.

As Abraham knew and as the Zohar has proclaimed, the Earth *is* the center of the universe, but at the metaphysical, not the physical, level. That is why, search as we will with increasingly vast arrays of radio telescopes, we never will find physical intelligences such as we are in other solar systems or other galaxies. Noncorporeal intelligences, on the other hand, proliferate there, and some of them dwarf our feeble intellect.

There was nothing wrong with Aristotle's methodology. He reasoned that the function of inanimate matter inevitably must revolve around the Earth because it was the only plain on which he could physically observe intelligence. Since that observation appeared to be supported by an external appearance indicating that celestial bodies do move about the Earth, his conclusion was impeccably logical. From the beginning, however, Abraham possessed the knowledge extant in the Book of Formation, and that knowledge directed him to the internal, metaphysical cosmic energy field, rather than to its external counterpart. He *was* certain, but neither as a scientist nor as a religionist, neither of which to this day have come to grips with the fact that every action of mankind has an equal, opposite reaction in cosmos, which makes the Earth and its remarkable inhabitants the true center of the universe regardless of what revolves around what.

There are several spiritual paths by which the metaphysical universe may be explored. They involve varying levels of consciousness and they connect with cosmic energy fields that can increase our awareness and elevate our enlightenment. The instrument used for this journey by the Sefir Yetzira and the Zohar is the Bible which, from the Kabbalistic point of view, is the one spiritual path by which achievement of pure awareness and cosmic consciousness may be achieved. The Bible, therefore, is not merely the document of a religion but the instrument, the medium, by which we can achieve the objective of connecting with cosmic energy fields.

The Zohar[119] cites the verse: "And Abraham took another wife and her name was Keturah...and Abraham gave all that he had unto Isaac, but unto the sons of the concubines that Abraham had, meaning the children of Keturah, Abraham gave gifts and sent them away from Isaac, his son, while he yet lived, eastward unto the East country."[120] The Zohar then asks how Abraham could have had anything to give to the sons of the concubine after giving all that he had to Isaac? The Zohar also raises the question of why the verse stresses where Abraham sent the sons of the concubine — eastward, into an eastern country. The Zohar explains that the gifts under consideration were spiritual paths, the highest of which were transmitted to Isaac and the lower of which were given to his half- brothers. They then were sent "eastward into an eastern country" where they founded the impure practice of magic and witchcraft. Isaac, alone, possessed the complete metaphysical system that elevated him to his rightful grade.

It is written, "and Solomon's wisdom excelled the wisdom of all the children of the east."[121] "Herein," says the Zohar, "is an allusion to the descendents of the very children of Abraham's concubine, who as is already said inhabit the mountains of the east where they instruct the sons of men in the arts of magic and divination. It was this very land of the east from which came Labon and Beor and his son Balaam who are all magicians."

The spiritual path given to Isaac was, of course, the three-column system described in detail in Kabbalah for the Layman[122] and reflected by the Star of David. The incomplete system borne eastward by the sons of the concubines was a two-column system and, to this day, eastern metaphysical systems are based on duality — Yin and Yang, left and right. To brand them "lower" is more than just an ego trip from those who possess the three-column system. The two are as different as Newtonian classical physics and Einsteinian physics. Newton's laws remain valid, but Einstein elevated science to a broader, more encompassing, level. Newton discussed mass, but lacking knowledge of the atom, his discussion dealt with the external. Einstein, with what could be called a "complete" scientific system, took physics inside the atom itself, and it is no surprise to the Kabbalist that the atom consisting of a triad of protons, neutrons and electrons, reflects the three-column system of Abraham. As Einstein was to do many millenia later, Abraham, in his Book of Formation, dealt with the internal aspects of cosmology, whereas eastern systems, which actually ranged from China to Egypt, dealt with the externals of astral influences and celestial bodies.

Thus it is easy to see how so wise a man as Aristotle could conclude that the Earth was the center of the universe. Just as Newtonian classical physics had its day, so did the aspect of eastern astrology. The Sefir Yetsira does not have to wait until tomorrow. It has been with us for a very long time, but to an individual like Aristotle, that sort of knowledge was concealed, just as Einsteinian physics was concealed from Newton. It is within the spiritual path, dealing with the internal, that Abraham shared with Isaac, where the heavy action really takes place, even to this day.

Unfortunately, the way the present scientific establishment is growing, it is becoming increasingly fossilized by its own particular world view. One cannot continue to create formulas and inject the ever increasing aspect of uncertainty at the same time. This begins to limit our growth and increase a specialization that threatens the sense of wholeness. The purpose of our being also has been severely fragmented by individual egos, which come to make the scientific empire an individual power base created by the owners of scientific knowledge they, themselves, have created. When the majority of the people are placed beyond grasp of true knowledge, then we are truly awaiting the messianic, or Aquarian age in which knowledge shall be the domain of all, not a select few. The Kabbalah, itself, has been a jealously guarded secret, but the time has come for it to reach the masses with its simplicity, because in the final analysis, knowledge which is simple is true knowledge. As stated in Jeremiah, "And they shall teach no more every man his neighbor, and every man his brother, saying, know the Lord. Rather everyone shall know Me, from the smallest to the hightest."[123]

The purpose, therefore, of the Zohar's explanation of the gifts of Abraham is not to engender a prejudicial attitude toward other paths in the field of astrology and astronomy, but rather to indicate that at this point in history, things have changed. Knowledge no longer is the same knowledge originally received by Abraham, and it is fortunate for us that a fresh approach to science in general and to the fields of astronomy and astrology in particular now can take place. This book is for people who no longer wish to tolerate a state of ambiguity — for those who truly understand that change is necessary and are not afraid of handling simple, if not yet accepted, ideas, These ideas will provide more answers than conventional information ever will bring.

For those who feel comfortable with eastern spiritual teachings and who have found their paths adequate for what they seek in life, more power to them, but from a Zoharic viewpoint, the purpose of King Solomon's declaration was to provide information about a system that will, hopefully, stimulate the thinking process and implant some new ideas in the minds, not only of scientist, but laymen as well. We now must begin to review our universe and build a new concept of it that deals with a holistic picture, rather than something that can encompass only the fragmented view of a particular scientist who deals with it exclusively on a physical, observable plane.

Our technological performance over the past 20 years really is, in effect, the evolution of intelligence itself. When we speak of "knowing," as in the Biblical phrase, "Adam knew Eve,"[124] we speak of connection. This is intelligence of that subtle stage known as cosmic consciousness. It reaches into the subatomic levels of energy, yet the average human cannot grasp more than 5 to 8 percent of his inherent intellectual capacity and the average scientist does little to overcome that limitation. Instead, he has relegated man to a position inferior to that modern Golem, the computer. We have come to believe that machine intelligence can solve most of our problems, and that with the computer, we are augmenting our own intelligence. As we continue to upgrade the state of the art in construction of computers, this sense of amplification will increase. One can predict with accuracy that the ultimate demise of all sciences will result in total acquiescence to the computer, at which time it finally will suffer ultimate breakdown. In the long run, the Golem — in Jewish folklore, a creature made of mud and animated by magic, but devoid of intelligence — will not be able to handle anything that man cannot handle.

Hopefully, in the near future, we will come to understand that each subatomic particle in the universe is as intelligent as a human being, because the internal activity of a particle is nothing more than an intelligence that directs the movement of the particle. These tiny intelligences eventually evolved into stars, planets, animals and people. Therefore, at that original atomic level, everyone knew everything and every thing knew every one.

Scientists insist that the evolutionary process follows very strict rules and operates in a highly structured manner and that therefore we eventually will come face to face with an alien life form very similar to ourselves. From the Kabbalistic point of view, this will never happen because the Earth and its chief occupant, man, are unique in the cosmos. Stars and other planets evolved from the seven basic elements and each of them operates within its own frame of reference. Consequently, none are alike, even at the atomic level of intelligence, and there can be no creatures like us any more than members of our own animal kingdom can be like *Homo sapiens*. Cats never will speak or dogs run for office because while cats, dogs and people occupy the same area, they operate on metaphysical levels that are light years apart.

For those who believe that the evolutionary process that governs this planet governs all and therefore will produce the same sort of creatures, including humankind, in other solar systems, we shall, in our next chapter, develop the theory of different intelligences and of the particular intelligence of earth itself. We will show that *Homo sapiens* did not simply evolve. The species exists because it is the exact composite of particular astral influences.

8

The Calendar

I know not whether Laws be right,
Or whether Laws be wrong;
All that we know who lie in gaol
Is that the wall is strong;
And that each day is like a year,
A year whose days are long.
— Oscar Wilde, "The Ballad of Reading Gaol"

T HE CALENDAR IS EVERYWHERE. IT HANGS IN THE KITCHEN, SITS on the office desk, nestles with myriad appointments in the businessman's breast pocket and rides in blinking digital numbers on the face of the modern watch. Without it, we would be lost in the trackless stream of linear time, condemned like a man in a jail cell to a perception in which days, months and years all become one — monotonous, undifferentiated and unending. We live, robotically, by the calendar, and we accept it so for granted that we haven't a clue as to its real significance.

The average person is aware, if he bothers to think of it, only that the calendar is structured around orbital flights of the Earth and Moon and, by measuring them, divides time into usable fragments. If the celestial bodies provided nothing more than a time table, however, the internal secrets of our celestial bodies would remain unrevealed. So profound is the affect of the calendar upon our lives that no less than three such systems have been devised, and they separate the cultures that use them as distinctly as they separate days, weeks and months. It therefore is essential in any study of astrology and astronomy to understand their structures.

The most widely used system, in the Western world at least, is the solar calendar which defines a year as the time taken by the earth to complete one orbit around the Sun — 365½ days. The solar calendar was originated by Julius Caesar in 46 BC and was refined as the Gregorian calendar in England in 1752. The second system is based on the revolution of the Moon around the Earth. The Moslem calendar is completely lunar in nature inasmuch as it is comprised of 12 months or 29 or 30 days. The lunar year, or the passing of 12 new moons, comes to approximately 354 days. With the solar calendar, the position of the Sun in conjunction with the seasons always is the same.

If we use the lunar system, however, any given month may, depending upon the year, fall during any of the solar seasons. As a result, no Moslem holiday will occur during the same season. Inasmuch as the length of the solar year is 365 days, five hours and 48 minutes while the length of a lunar month is 29 days, 12 hours and 44 minutes, the solar year exceeds the 12 lunar months by about 11 days. In the course of just a few years, the total difference becomes considerable and causes the beginning of each lunar year to wander through different seasons of the solar system. Since each year, the end of 12 lunar months precedes the end of the solar year by 11 days, in 20 years, a holiday that occurs at the end of the lunar year ultimately will occur 211 days before the end of the solar year, or seven months before Jan. 1.

The third calendar is the lunar/solar system unpon which the Jewish calendar is based. This calendar is based solely neither upon the lunar nor the solar year, but reconciles the two into a mode of calculation in which months are reckoned according to the moon while years are calculated according to the Sun. Since all Jewish holidays and festivals occur on days mandated by the Bible according to the lunar month, the lunar year must be reconciled with the solar system to prevent holidays form wandering through the solar period. Thus, Passover always will occur during the spring and Rosh Hashanna, the Jewish new year, in late summer or early autumn. This differs from the Moslem calendar where festivals drift through different seasons. Under that system, in the beginning, the lunar month of Aries would correspond to the solar month of Aries, but the following year, the lunar month of Aries would begin 11 days earlier, eventually drifting through fall, then back through summer.

The reconciliation of lunar months and seasons of the solar year on the Jewish calendar is accomplished by intercalation. By adding an extra month, known as the intercalary month, seven times in every 19 years, the lunar months become adjusted with the seasons of the solar year. Consequently, the 14th day of the Hebrew month of Nissan, or Passover, personifying the cosmic energy force of Aries, never will occur prior to the sun sign of Aries, which is March 20 through April 23, the terminating date of Aries. This remarkable mathematical calculation of intercalation, provided by Rabbinic scholars, demonstrates the enormous importance that our solar system, along with its astral influences, reflect in the lives of all intelligences in this universe.

It might well be asked why the Judaic world should go to the trouble of intercalation when it might be simpler merely to adopt the Gregorian calendar, with its precisely fixed days and let it go at that. To do so, however, would be to abandon a very specific mechanism within the lunar/solar calendar which the Gregorian calendar does not have. Again—the calendar is more than merely a time-table for the schedules of men.

Taken on such a broad scale as that presented by the Jewish calendar, contemplation of the universe as a structure beyond the limits of physical science does not seem so strange, nor does the concept of cosmic influences as a mathematical formula or the idea of marriage as an electrical circuit. When it became necessary to add an extra month in seven of every 19 years, the sum of months contained in those seven years, with each year composed of 13 months, adds up to 91 months. The figure 91, and the total of intervening days between each season, which also is 91, has, from a Kabbalistic point of view, profound implications. Translated to the Hebrew language, it emerges as "Amen," the word with which Jews and Christians alike end prayer. The word is a plea for atonement, or, hyphenated for the sake of understanding, "at-one-ment." It asks, in short, for the blessing of connection, which is what Kabbalah is all about.

The movement of celestial bodies did not, however, cause the resulting number to be 91. Rather, the significance of 91 is a coded mathematical formula which expresses a specific internal cosmic energy force with a potential astral influence upon our universe.

The physical orbital interplay between the Sun, Moon and Earth is the result of a higher cosmic intelligence that is the motivation of physically expressed orbital interrelationships. From a subatomic point of view, all physically expressed orbital entities — the body of a man, for example — are merely the evolvement of prior metaphysically motivated intelligences. If serious moral and ethical changes are to be forthcoming, they must begin with a dramatic change in man's view of his environment. The human physical reality does not become motivated without a prior motivating thought. We must condition ourselves to viewing the entire universe within the same frame of reference. The physical expression can influence the prior, caused, aspect no more than the physical body of man can affect the original DNA.

Let us return to the original commandment, "Observe the month of Abib, and keep the Passover unto the Lord, for in this month of Abib, the Lord brought thee forth out of Egypt by night," to find what brought about the need to reconcile the lunar system with the seasons of the solar system.

Why the month of Abib? Abib is the season of spring, when green things begin to bud or break out of winter's bondage. Abib is the season of freedom. It is not by accident that the slang term for aiding and abetting a jail break is to "spring" the prisoner. Spring is Aries and Aries is the beginning; only in the month of Abib could freedom begin for the Israelites.

Commandments or mandates of the Bible, from a Kabbalistic point of view, are not treated within the framework of religion or tradition. They are considered for their cosmic significance and importance. The Biblical requirement that the lunar system coincide and become reconciled with the seasons of the solar year therefore must be understood within a cosmic frame of reference.

What seems to emerge from this particular section of the Bible is that if the lunar months were permitted to go retrograde through the seasons, carrying particular Jewish holidays, including Passover, with them, then the cosmic conjunction event of lunar-solar might never have happened. This fascinating panorama of cosmic interplay provided the setting for the great Exodus which occurred amid an awful upheaval that ultimately terminated the incredible and awesome period of Egyptian history and power.[126] This meant that the Jew now could tap the cosmic energy field produced as a result of this cosmic conjunction and destroy the negative cosmic energy force that enslaved the known world.[127]

The Biblical description of the scope of the catastrophe, accompanied by the ten plagues,[128] which personified the forces of the cosmic drama, was not intended merely to record so startling and revolutionary a story, but to demonstrate the kind of cosmic energy that is made available for us to tap and capture for our own benefit.

During the period of the Exodus, a pessimistic outlook about the future was prevalent throughout the world because of the complete estrangement, or negation, of freedom in the form of the internal aspect of the all-inclusive positive energy source. Man, when connected to this positive cosmic energy force, is not a slave to the desire to receive for himself alone, but rather can encompass an entire universe, feeling togetherness with everything in it, including his fellow man. The desire to receive for the self alone is the energy of technology and since that is what slavery is all about, the same mood prevails today as that which brooded over the great Exodus.

The followers of Moses were slaves to material energy, but it had the same base — desire to receive for the self alone. The time came in which the world would be freed through destruction of this empiracal force at its metaphysical level during the Middle Kingdom of Egypt. Today, we see the same slavery to technological energy under which we have become completely bound up with computers. We have become so programmed that we can't think independently and we have become so involved with what we cannot do that we are virtually paralyzed.

Happily, we enter the mood of Exodus in the Age of Aquarius. We are ready for freedom and that freedom can only come about when we can get in once again to tap the original power source: The internal aspect of cosmic energy. That is why the Jewish calendar is so important.

The Bible refers to the month of Aries as the "Rosh," or head:[129] "And this month shall be unto you the Rosh of the months." Rosh also means beginning, and though "head" and "beginning" are not synonymous, for our purposes they are indicative of the same thing. At a physical, mundane level, no individual can make manifest any action until he has thought about what he is going to do. After the thinking process has been completed, it then is executed and put into motion.

This is the purpose of the "Rosh," the head; that action taken in this particular month will make manifest all subsequent manifestations on a cosmic level for the next 11 months. This is the secret that was revealed through the Zohar. This is the head, the beginning.

The day of massive practical application in tapping the power source lay far in the future in Abraham's day. The concepts it contained, although already mentioned in the Sefer Yetzirah, were for Abraham. He could make use of them, but Judah would have to wait until the time of the Exodus. Now we return to a question asked earlier: Why was the precept of sanctifying the new moon mentioned just prior to the tenth plague, which was the plague of the first born? The first-born possess Rosh energy, a concept more fully explained in "The Kabbalah Connection,"[130] and, for the Jew, it was imperative to destroy the head of Egyptian power and force so that it never again would revert to the energy force that enslaved Israel.

Today, we find ourselves dominated by this energy force again, but it is not equal, nor should it be compared, to the energy force that the Egyptians displayed and controlled at the time of the Exodus. Today, it is called, in the common vernacular, "High Tech." The Egyptians had the "Valley of Kings," with its marvels of pyramids, embalming and "magic." We have Silicon Valley, where microchips are made to function as only the human mind functioned before. To insure a complete safe and free future, a complete removal of the dominance of energy matter, which pertains to the desire to receive for itself alone, is necessary. We must return to the ultimate computer, the human brain. Anything else is surrender. To physically escape that which dominates the world landscape is, of course, impossible. The highest mountains of Tibet, the wildest deserts of Outer Mongolia, have been invaded at this point by the microchip in one incarnation or another, but if we yield to the negative aspects of high tech, eventually we will have to pay the price of the Golem.

This point recently was explored by author Whitley Streiber in a terrifying futuristic novel titled "Warday." It recounts what passes for life in a balkanized United States following a limited nuclear war not vast enough to trigger nuclear winter and annihilate all life, but enough to destroy both the United States and the Soviet Union and make them poor vessals of the surviving superpowers of Britain and Japan. In "Warday," it is neither the destruction of a few cities nor the famine and plague that follow that destroys the United States. It is high-voltage "electromagnetic pulse" from a couple of 50-megaton bombs detonated well above the Earth's atmosphere to destroy, in the blink of an eye, every computer system upon which the fabric of our lives depends.

The microchip-created Golem, to which we had surrendered all records, all history, all the mechanics of production and social interaction, fell, and we fell with it. Streiber may prove to be a modern prophet.

The scientific basis for all of the advanced technology that we know today has brought with it problems many people feel probably are insoluble. Under the impact of computer technology, we ultimately run the risk of becoming so inundated with information that our very survival may be in jeopardy. Computer technology has brought us a great deal of benefit, but so ubiquitous has it become that any serious breakdown could cripple an entire country. At the time of Exodus, a specific date within the month of Aries, a confrontation occurred between two internal energy forces which were not represented by physical matter, but were so potent that when the event occurred, through Jewish knowledge of cosmology, it destroyed the head of material energy that existed as desire to receive for the self alone. The same sort of confrontation, with a level of equal impact on future generations, is pending and it will give those of us who can learn to wield its power the ability to remain free.

This early version of "Star Wars" took place in the days of Moses and the Jew was given information by which he ultimately would be the victor. He was going to win by tapping the all-inclusive positive energy to subjugate the negative energy that had kept him in bondage. We know, as described in "Kabbalah for the Layman,"[131] that the all-inclusive positive energy came first, and when it is tapped, darkness is banished and the enemies who rule through the negative energy of desire to receive for oneself alone is overthrown. Such bondage was not exclusive to Moses' day. It still reigns, if not always so brutally, in our time, but as always, once the all-inclusive positive energy is established, it automatically does away with the negative force which is the root of all evil in the universe.

Enter a darkened room and light a match and you've done away with darkness. It's that simple. The two do not appear together. Light is not merely the absence of darkness, nor is darkness the absence of light. Darkness is a very potent cosmic energy force as the Zohar makes clear: "In the beginning, in the Ain Sof, there was no coloring of any kind whatsoever. Neither white, neither black, neither green, neither red. No coloring whatsoever."[132] We learn from the Zohar that each color represents an internal energy force, and that includes black. Consequently, when the cosmic energy of the all-inclusive positive energy is prevalent, it removes the internal energy force of darkness, which was the internal energy force of the Egyptians.

The Biblical battle between the forces of light and darkness, when the Jew was given the three-column system discussed in detail in "Kabbalah for the Layman"[133] and revealed in Exodus,[134] ("And they shall take of the blood and put it on the two side posts and the lintel upon the houses wherein they shall eat.") is emphasized here because it has bearing on events that were to come millennia after the Exodus.

The Jews in Egypt slaughtered the lamb, the blood of which was designed to turn aside the Angel of Death, as the Sun was going down indicating that the transfer of cosmic energy intelligence that produces the metaphysical DNA for negative, destructive, energy flow, takes place at this particular time. The story of Exodus lies now in the mists of history, but the time correlation remains the same today as it was then.

For Abraham, the Exodus and modern man, timing was and is of the essence, whether modern man consciously knows it or not. If one changes a metaphysical DNA, that which already has been designated by the DNA also is changed. One thus may alter the course and consequences of a year, or even of a lifetime. The timing of an event is equally important when knowledge of the information process being transferred or transmitted at a particular time is available. Therefore, the essential timing of Exodus, as stated in the Zohar,[135] was on the 10th and 14 days of Nissan.

A negative cosmic energy field and negative cosmic terminals are functional at the setting of the Sun. Consequently, when Abraham received information concerning the exiles and saw that the Jew in the future would have to suffer, he received a metaphysical DNA prediction. This does not mean, however, that such predictions could not have been altered. They could have, had the Jew subsequently made use of the information at hand. His own particular cosmic energy field contained a composite of the three-column system in which his desire to receive for himself alone was harnessed and placed into a triad. When the triad position of the circular concept effectively has been reached, an altered state of consciousness has been achieved. The result of this new frame of reference is to provide a changed, higher, parallel level of existence where a completely new set of rules and principles now govern. A new program, to speak in the vernacular of the computer, has been entered into the corporeal "main frame" of the individual. A computer carries a program which can be updated from time to time without altering the physical state of the computer. The same holds true with a human. While his body does not seem to have undergone change, a new metaphysical DNA, with all its subsequent ramifications, can become manifest. This is the parallel level of existence — parallel because some original aspects and cosmic energy, the physical structure for example, remain the same.

The Jew, at the time of the great Exodus, made the outer space connection. In so doing, he left behind his entire prior existence, along with its programmed metaphysical DNA. He no longer retained the state of cosmic energy that was dominated by the priesthood of Egypt. The program had been changed because the Jews had learned how to connect with and tap cosmic energy from the all inclusive positive energy by transforming their very essence and being. The Jewish people had taken a leap forward to another state of cosmic consciousness, leaving behind the level of consciousness of a multi-incarnated soul.

The fall of Adam predetermined the metaphysical DNA of intelligence, creating the cosmic soul presence of the deluge, the Tower of Babel, the generations of the great Exodus and the repeated appearance of souls reincarnated for those very events.[136] For the very first time, the altering of a metaphysical DNA had been accomplished by a nation as a whole. In the past, this almost impossible feat had been reserved for the select few. With Exodus, a celestial cosmic event of vast magnitude had been established within the cosmos, never again to be lost, but to remain eternally for future generations to tap. Even now, it provides an opportunity to change the predetermined, predestined, metaphysical DNA to which the particular cosmic intelligence of the reincarnated soul previously had been programmed. No longer would humanity be compelled to live by the agonies of a predetermined programming triggered by the incarnated cosmic soul. Through knowledge, plus the determination to upgrade one's cosmic spiritual level to an altered state of consciousness, this change of DNA now was possible. It should, however, be made crystal clear that if a decision to upgrade one's level of spirituality or spiritual growth has not been formulated, then knowledge and connection cannot and will not serve as a substitute for internal spiritual progress.

Over the centuries, the Jews, themselves, learned this and wept. The race, that by the hand of the Almighty once had the power to bring mighty Egypt to its knees and eventually to march through the promised land virtually immune to the warlike resistance of its inhabitants, was to suffer subsequent centuries of diaspora, persecution, suffering and, eventually, the nightmare of the holocaust. All of these events occurred simply because they let slip the level of spirituality and hence command of the three-column system given to them under Moses. Even in the Bible, their slide began with creation of the Golden Calf and a rebellion against God that kept them wandering in the wilderness for 40 years before they were permitted to enter the promised land. But the power they once had still exists and it still can be tapped "between the evenings."[138]

Again, the Zohar[137] provides us with a clue as to what "between the evenings" means. The Zohar says, "Ha'rah signifies the one supernal crown which represents Egypt." That word, "Ha'rah," indicates the enormous power of the negative cosmic energy transmission that was represented by Egypt because it had the connection and knew how to tap that power source. The Zohar says the word "darkness" is a second such supernal crown of negative cosmic energy which was represented by the Babylonian exiles. The word "great" in the verse refers to the Edominte, or Roman, exile which was to be the longest and hardest of all.

"Thus it is seen," continues the Zohar, "that the Israelites did not go out of Egypt until all the supernal powers and principalities which were Israel's enemies had been brought to nought. But when these things had come to pass, the people were free from their domination and brought under the holy and heavenly sway of the Holy One, blessed be He, and were joined to Him and to Him alone, as it is written, "for unto Me, the children of Israel are servants. They are servants whom I brought forth out of the land of Egypt.[139] Thus, the final curtain on the great Middle Kingdom of Egypt came down.

Far out in interstellar space, celestial harmony seems to be the order of the day. During the day, we can see no planets at all since the sun is so much brighter to our eyes than they. We can study the celestial heavens from evening, and it is only then that we observe the beauty, the loneliness, power and the unspoken word that each one seems to offer.

It is difficult to know the truth about the origin of our planetary systems. The problems of beginning and evolvement of our celestial system suffers from an overdose of scientific prescription called speculation. Since we were not present when it all began, how can we legitimately come to any conclusions as to how and why it came about? Astronomers once thought all planets moved around the Earth in complicated orbits. This belief persisted until 1543 when the Polish astronomer Nicolaus Copernicus created his epoch-making breakthrough, showing that the planets, the Earth included, revolved around the Sun. Acceptance of this new way of thinking, however, did not really change people or the way they were to think about themselves in relation to the vast cosmic structure suddenly revealed.

The three types of calendrial systems formulated by civilizations to measure the passage of the time are highly sophisticated vehicles of great accuracy, pinpointing the solstices which give us our seasons, and other pertinent data concerning the day and night cycles which dominate the most import aspect of all Earth's realities. Our planet rotates from west to east. The Sun still is seen rising in the east and setting in the west. Little, in common daily reflection, has changed since the Copernican revolution. We take its function for granted; hang the calendar on the wall, and forget it. That, perhaps, is why even when we summarize all the data and evidence concerning the three basic calendar systems, we find that we still have not come to grips with Kabbalah's most important question: Why?

Is it merely by chance that the Western world accepted the Gregorian calendar, based on the solar system, while the Jews established one with a lunar-solar base and the Moslems opted only for a lunar measurement? Is there more to these events than meets the eye? Could there have been, and possibly still be, mitigating cosmic circumstances that have mandated this three-calendar matrix? Now that we have accustomed ourselves to questioning the obvious, removing the framework in which most of us have been cloaked through our educational system, we shall make an attempt to in-vestigate the motivating factors. First, let us probe the unseen metaphysical cosmic energy forces upon which these calendar systems are based and ask what cosmic intelligence dictated the West's acceptance of the Gregorian calendar.

The lunar month, which had served as the basis of many early calendars, was superceded in Roman times by Julius Caesar who created the Julian calendar in 46 B.C. Using the solar rotation as his model, Caesar fixed the length of the year at 365½ days, then decreed that every fourth year should have 366 days to take up the fractional slack. This calendar, however, proved to be out of step with the Sun, producing the error of one day every 128 years. Pope Gregory XIII came up with a new calendar in 1752 which necessitated the dropping of 10 days. As a result, Oct. 4 was immediately followed by Oct. 15. This calendar, known as the Gregorian, was adopted by England and the American colonies in 1752 and now is used throughout most parts of the western world.

The Moslem calendar is similar to the Chinese calendar except that it reckons time from July 16, A.D. 622. Entirely lunar in nature, the Moslem calendar is composed of 12 months of 29 or 30 days which wander through the solar seasons. Certainly a need must have been felt to stabilize this measurement of time and fix the days in orderly cycles dictated by the celestial bodies, but it never has been done. Is there, then, a metaphysical intelligence that has programmed the Moslem world not to adopt the more logical systems of the Gregorian and Hebrew calendars? Can we assume that some internal energy field central to the Moslem people directed their choice of a lunar system? The same question can be directed with respect to the Chinese lunar calendar which supposedly dates back to 2397 B.C. In any case, the Chinese calendar is different from the Moslem version only in that its months run between 28 and 30 days. The lunar-solar calendar of the Hebrews reckons time from the year of creation, 3761 B.C., a time frame generally accepted by fundamentalist Christians.

Such a date, set for the creation of all things, does, of course, collide head-on with antropological findings indicating mankind, in a more primitive mode, perhaps, may have occupied the Earth for as long as 1 million years, while fully developed Cro-Magnon men walked the landscapes of Europe 10,000 to 15,000 years ago. It is a collision, however, that will not bother the Kabbalist who is accustomed to dealing in different frames of reference and varying levels of consciousness. Suffice to say that fixing the date of Genesis by counting the ages given in the Bible for the patriarchs at their respective deaths is sufficient to create a working calendar whatever the system of its basis.

Neither celestial charts, sundials nor astronomical values established in different parts of the world, and essentially unchanged to the present time, can provide logical reasoning for the Jews, Chinese, Moslems or the Western world to choose their particular calendars. While stability of the calendar can, to a large degree, be attributed to the celestial order of our universe, reasons for the choices made remain a mystery.

On July 20, 1969, Apollo 11 astronauts became the first humans to set foot on the Moon. From that moment on, the Moon became one of the best known celestial bodies outside of Earth. When Neil Armstrong and Edwin Aldrin, Jr. returned, after making the first human footprints on the Moon, they brought scores of photographs and rock and soil samples. Scientists now would speculate about Earth-Moon history as never before and study the Moon's mineral content, but little else. The Moon, Earth's constant companion, unlocked some of the great mysteries of our universe, but it failed to answer the question of why the Earth has a constant companion in the first place. It is precisely this lack of understanding of the internal cosmic forces that exist within these two celestial entities that prevent a further in-depth probe of the Moon.

Nothing of real scientific value for humans seems to have emerged from this very expensive exploration of our constant companion. Unfortunately, science persists in the backward method of investigation, beginning its probe from a superficial physical level, then proceeding inward to the more subtle layers and dimension. Continuing our own investigation into the iternal, cosmic intelligence of the Moon, and following the principles of Kabbalistic interpenetration, we return again to exploring the particular calendrical systems adopted by the three various regions of our earthly universe in which the West chose the solar system, the East, or Moslem, the lunar, and Israel, in the center, the lunar-solar.

The ultimate, physical manifestation seen on a mundane level can tell many interesting things about oneself, about nations and even about parts of the universe. Such things are revealed by the manner in which astral influences reach out and connect with particular mundane vessels that seem to correspond and become reconciled with other particular mundane vessels that seem to correspond and become reconciled with other particular astral influences. Consequently, the Zohar, in providing us with in-depth penetration of internal astral influences and reconciling them with the internal aspects and characteristics of people, nations and universes, immediately provides us with this sort of information rather than forcing us to grope from a physical level as does the scientific community. The Kabbalistic world view[140] provides us with the root manifestations, thereby avoiding a great deal of the research and development that must go into the areas when we deal with matters on a physical plane, inasmuch as physicality has so many infinite layers that literally conceal that which is below. All technology and research can do in analyzing the seed of any particular plant or vegetable still will not reach much further than the superficial layers of these particular entities.

It is through profound study of the Zohar, which is based on the Bible and its narrations, that we gain this kind of internal sub-atomic perception that otherwise would be eternally blocked for us. What we would deal with when discussing the "why" of the particular segments of this universe and its population of intelligences, or the "why" of choosing particular calendrical systems, from a Kabbalistic world view, would be a very valid question.

Let us answer it first by exploring those cosmic intelligences that mandated acceptance by the Western world of the solar, or Gregorian, calendar.

Historically, the Western world is represented by Rome, which gave it the bulk of its law, its political methodology, its culture and even the root of its many languages. The Zohar considers Rome the left column of the klipot,[141] which is the aspect of world physicality, the aspect of negativity, the aspect of the electron. That Rome, and its nation descendants, was to be ruled by expansion of the metaphysical aspects of the left column is demonstrated by technological advances that represent a definement of the desire to receive for oneself alone.

The Gregorian calendar was accepted by the Western world

because the west is ruled by the Sun — the primary aspect of negativity, of fire and of the intense desire to receive. [142] Wherever there is an intense desire to receive, technological advancement will be manifest. When we speak of high-tech, better systems, more sophisticated hardware, we are, in effect, discussing the channels for transfer of energy, not the energy itself. These channels are the vessels that create physical expressions of energy. As noted before, that which we are transferring, the internal element, whether it be a television show, radio programming or the activation of a satellite in space — anyting and everthing that begins and becomes actualized in one place and appears elsewhere — has, at the moment of becoming actualized, already appeared metaphysically elsewhere and everywhere. The pressing of a button at any space center to activate a satellite is the secondary, or physical, expression of a thought process that cannot be revealed until it becomes clothed within a physical vessel.

In this case, the pressing of a button has become that vessel which teveals the thought of the individual who has decided to press the button. The physical transfer of the thought, which is the energy of internal intelligence, then appears to take place. The fact is that the internal intelligence already has activated the instrument in space by metaphysical means. The action in space remains in a passive, potential state, awaiting the activation of the physical vessel by means of the punched button to reveal the thought process.

This revolutionary outlook is comprehensible now by virtue of quantum mechanics which describes the universe as one interrelated whole. The deeper the scientist probes the universe, newly sophisticated detection devices will be developed. We will, in the forseeable future, be able to detect the thought process as an intelligent energy force transcending the limitations of space and time. The thought, which is a non-material energy force, will be seen as having pervaded the entire universe simultaneously, faster than the speed of light. Western high-tech is headed toward instantaneous, faster-than-light vessels, or channels, that will immediately reveal intelligent erergy forces at the metaphysical level. This leaves us with an exciting note that belongs, for the moment at least, in the realm of science fiction: instantaneous transfer of matter, such as a populated star ship, from the vicinity of planet Earth to Barnard's Star or Alpha Centauri. Scoffers should be reminded that all space travel — including that which took us to the Moon in the Apollo program and that which now takes us into orbit aboard the space shuttle as readily as a Greyhound bus will take us to Kansas City — once lay in the realm of science fiction. The fact is, if we are on a correct path, both physically and metaphysically, there is nothing wonderful at all about such a concept.

Atoms are all around us, but they remain in a passive, potential state until a vessel or channel reveals and makes them manifest. A chair or the wall of a house are no more than a composite of atoms which become manifest by the physical vessel known as wood or stone. From a Kabbalistic point of view, atoms are forms of intelligence, the electron the desire to receive, the proton as the desire to share, the neutron as the desire to restrict. They contain all the interrelated aspects that act as metaphysical conveyances of our thought processes. Stretching this concept one step further, when a person wishes to throw a stone at a window, the glass already has received this information by means of the activating thought process that transcends space and time. The internal process of shattering thus begins long before the actual physical act of impact takes place. If the stone ultimately does not reach the glass, the internal, metaphysical, process of shattering neither will begin or take place.

The research and development of highly sophisticated systems for the transfer of energy, which is nothing more than intelligence, thus lies within the domain of the West.

It does not, nor will it ever, lie within the grasp of the East, where the lunar calendar prevails, with one exception: Japan is part of the East, yet the Japanese have proven their ability to develop highly sophisticated systems based on the technological desire to receive. This is explanable by Japan's own historical self-definition as "the land of the rising sun," or "Nippon," which means "land of the origin of the sun." For all of its geographical and cultural links with the East, Japan has been metaphysically aligned with the West for centuries.

The desire to receive, which is more fully explained in "Kabbalah for the Layman,"[143] indicates motivation — a drive that depends upon intensity. The greater the intensity of that desire, the greater the ambition and, as a byproduct, the possibility of more intense selfishness and greater power for evil. The Roman Empire displayed those negative characteristics as did no nation before it. Romans of the totally materialistic imperial period boasted that "All roads lead to Rome," and, in a fine display of the desire to receive for the self alone, indeed they did. It therefore is no wonder that Rome and the Western world that followed it adopted the Gregorian calendar, based upon the Sun and the negative, left column of the three-column system.

Nor is it any wonder that the East, dominated by the Moslem world, adopted the pure lunar calendar. The Zohar spells it out: "The children of Ishmael will at the same time rouse all the people of the world to come up to war against Jerusalem[144]. . .for I will gather all nations to war against Jerusalem to battle[145]. . . ." Ishmael is the right column of the klippot[146] — the aspect of positivity, the aspect of the proton, which rarely, if ever, is in action. The lunar system, which is the aspect of water, where Leo, or fire, is ruled by the Sun and Cancer, or water, is the right column ruled by the Crab, which, in turn, is ruled by the Moon. This right column is typified by static immobility. It indicates desire to receive for the sake of sharing, and that virtue always has been characteristic of the Arab. Even today, his hospitality, his warmth to strangers, his love of sharing is legendary. He is of the right column and his society never will embrace high technology. From the beginning, cosmic intelligence mandated that he would follow a lunar calendar with no regard to shifting days and seasons.

This leaves only the central column of the three-column system, and there, in manifestation of the desire to restrict, lives Israel. Of Israel, the Zohar says: "And all the children of Israel will assemble in their various places until the completion of the century. The Vav will then join the Hay and "they shall bring all your brethern out of all the nations for an offering unto the Lord.'"[148]

Only through the central column can there be an ultimate joining of the left and the right for a positive expression of the all-embracing unification. Only the Jew, who all too often through history has forgotten the system given to his forefathers at the time of Exodus, but who ultimately will remember it, can bring such unification about.

Did the Jew then choose the lunar-solar calendar? Or did the lunar-solar calendar choose him? The answer is obvious.

The calendar system, then, was neither an accident of creation nor the product of whimsy, and neither is an individual's life. It does not consist of a series of "coincidences" and chance encounters. When we study Kabbalistic astrology, we not only have to learn about the physical nature of the universe, but we also must make contact with the metaphysical aspects of it. The two aspects, astronomy and astrology, must work together if a more comprehensive world view of the universe is to be achieved. The Kabbalah provides the underlying universal laws and patterns, which science ultimately defines in their peculiar way — the manifestations of the physical universe. We should, however, always bear in mind that the physical universe is not the only plane of consciousness and intelligence. There are infinite and visible levels of energy upon which the process of creation always is at work.

These infinite metaphysical levels, unfortunately, so undetected by modern instruments of the physical sciences. This book in particular, and the Kabbalah in general, seeks in some way to prepare the individual and lead him into an expansion of the consciousness. The first step toward that goal is to understand that what we are referring to are not concepts beyond the reach and realm of science. Let us not forget that microbes and single-celled animals were in an invisible world until the invention of the microscope, and that some of our solar system's planets remained in an unknown world until the invention of the telescope. X-rays and cosmic rays were the stuff of science fiction and fantasy until we developed instruments to measure them and make them manifest.

As science evolves and more things become visible, we never should forget that it is still the physical scientist who somehow never seems to be overly concerned about *how* things come into being. This, I believe, is the vital role that Kabbalah plays in providing a total picture of the scheme of things, then, through the physical sciences, understanding the processes by which these initial rules of intelligence and evolution became manifest.

The principles of Kabbalah, being spiritual, must of necessity transcend the notions of independent, private prejudices or delusions of racial superiority. Ultimately, the student of Kabbalah will have the opportunity to rise above those beliefs, engraved from childhood, and become uplifted by a spiritual light—the Light of Wisdom.

Mankind always has been divided into various ethnic groups, and each race has developed according to its own kind of civilization. Man reveals through the evolutionary process on a physical, mundane level a diversity that continues today, with some nations rising and some nations falling, but the internal aspect is what governs the ultimate variations and self-expressions. Man can be united if there is an understanding that at the root level, man is unified, if not exactly "created equal." We are not created equal, but that does not mean that one man is more important than another. The more expansive our cosmic consciousness becomes, the more we will recognize the harmony and direct relationships between ourselves and the process of evolution of the universe as a whole. Then man can come to live with his fellow man, provided each individual understands the all-embracing unity of harmony which exists in a diversity under which each one is independent, yet interdependent, upon the other.

Now we come to a revealing Zohar that concerns itself with the days of the Aquarius-Messianic period: "In the year 73, all the kings of the world will assemble in the great city of Rome. And the Lord shall cause celestial collisions and will shower on them fire and hail and meteor stones until they are all destroyed, with the exception of those who will not yet have arrived there."[149] It is a divinely orchestrated catastrophe showing the interrelationship of man and the universe. Is it prophecy? Possibly. Could it find grim application to the United States in years to come? One thing alone is certain. The aspect of sharing, which this country has displayed as has no nation in history from the great waves of immigration through the rebuilding of Japan and Germany after World War II, is what has made a superpower of the United States. If ever we lose that aspect, we can expect to fall as surely as Rome and Egypt did.

Several instances related in scripture commemorate great cosmic phenomena, when forces of the universe are directly related to the termination of kingdoms. Another example:

"R. Isaac once drew close to the foot of a mountain and there saw a man sleeping under a tree. R. Isaac sat down. Suddenly, and without warning, the Earth began to quake violently and became full of fissures. The tree was uprooted and fell to the ground and the man beneath it woke and cried with a loud voice: "The quaking of the Earth signals a warning to you that a new ruler is being appointed in Heaven who will cause great misfortune to Israel.'"[150]

The cosmic catastrophe discribed in the Zohar is similar to the one mentioned in the Book of Joshua:[151]

"The Earth underwent a bombardment of hail and stones: "As they fled from before Israel, and they were going down to Beth-Horon, the Lord cast down great stones from Heaven upon them and they died. There were more dead from hail stones than they who died by the sword of Israel."

The meteor stones fell in great numbers inasmuch as more people died in the torrent than were slain by the forces of Israel. Does such a cataclysm happen to mark the end of some point in history? In truth, just such a phenomenon previously had taken place to bring about the end of a great kingdom, the Middle Kingdom of Egypt during the Great Exodus: "There fell an awesome hail, such as had not been in Egypt since its beginning.[152] These stones fell mingled with fire."[153] The Talmud states that the stones which fell on Egypt were hot,[154] fitting the description mentioned in the Zohar. The story of the revolt of Korah and his party contains a reference to cosmic upheaval: "And the Earth opened her mouth and swallowed them up. All Israel that were around them fled at their cry and there came out a fire from the Lord and consumed the two hundred and fifty men that offered incense."[155]

Similar descriptions come from various places mentioned in the Book of Prophets in which the destiny and fortunes of nations relate to great catastrophes. Isaiah received the awesome mission of prophesying the destruction of the Babylonian empire and spoke in terms of awful cosmic movements in the cosmos: "For the stars of Heaven and their constellations shall not give their light. Therefore I shall shake the Heavens and the Earth shall remove out of her place in the wrath of the Lord and in the day of His fierce anger."[156] It does appear that with the fall of the Babylonian kingdom, a cosmic event or change took place within the celestial nature of the stars in heaven, the light of the Moon and Sun and, more startling, that the Earth moved away from its center. Isaiah speaks in a similar manner when portraying the loss of the land of Israel to Sennacherib: "The foundations of the Earth do shake, the Earth is utterly broken down, the Earth is clean dissolved, the Earth is moved exceddingly. The Earth shall reel to and fro like a drunkard."[157]

What seems to emerge from these scriptures is that they contain an account of the interrelationship between what befalls the Heavens or altering of the given order of our universe, the Earth's rotation and the rise and fall of kindgoms, or, in a more subtle frame or reference, the rise and fall of the individual. What I have endeavored to show in citing such scriptures is that cosmic upheaval and cosmic determinations and influences have some connection with the actions of man. Was Joshua's miracle in stopping the Sun then a natural phenomenon, or does man actually have the ability to move and motivate stars, repel their negative influences and tap their positive energy forces?

The scriptural descriptions of cosmic catastrophe indicate a need for a new approach to celestial mechanics. What has become apparent is that the ultimate determining factor of cosmic upheaval is directly linked to the actions of man. This revolutionary viewpoint makes it possible to understand the evolutionary process of transition of Judaism from a cosmic religion, involving planet worship, to the concept of monotheism with its idea of the all inclusive positive energy force which is the desire to share — in short, the Creator.

This is how and why the Jewish people, starting with the patriarch, Abraham, were able to cast off their early belief in the deity of the stars, shared with other nations, and embrace the one, all-inclusive God. Abraham received the knowledge of astral influences in its entirety, with the conclusion that it was to the internal positive energy force that we were to connect and tap, and not the external intelligence of the negative energy force. As stated in the Zohar,[158] when a nation has succumbed and worships the aspect of negative intelligence, then we can expect cosmic upheaval which is the result of that nation's connection to the negative energy forces and their worship. Worship can assume many forms—even the worship of technology.

9

The Cosmic Calendar: Predestination?

"And he said in the sight of Israel, 'Sun, stand still upon Gibeon, and, Moon, stay in the valley of Ajalon.' And the Sun stood still, and the Moon stayed until the people had avenged themselves upon their enemies."

—Joshua, 10:12-14

PROBABLY THE MOST BIZARRE AND INCREDIBLE STORY OF COSMIC miracles is the one that marked the career of the successor of Moses, Joshua Ben Nun. While pursuing the Amorites at Beth-Horon, he directed the Sun and the Moon to stand still, and they did it, we are told, for the course of a whole day so that an Israelite victory could be assured: "For the Lord hearkened unto the voice of a man. For the Lord fought for Israel."[159]

Are we then to assume, on the basis of the Book of Joshua, that at some time during the middle of the second millenium the Earth's rotation about the Sun was interrupted by the command of a mortal man? Joshua, speaking to the Lord, implored this startling cosmic disruption before the eyes of Israel, and these celestial bodies, whose cosmic

DNA of energy dictates that they move along their precise, predestined, orbital paths, obeyed as if this very interruption was cosmically present in their computerized program from the time of their creation,[160] and indeed it was. Joshua's halting of the Sun and the Moon was no different than Moses' parting of the Red Sea as the Zohar indicates:

"Said Rabbi Isaac, "In that hour when the Israelites drew near to the sea, the Lord summoned the great angel appointed over the sea and said: 'When I created the world I appointed you over the sea, making at the same time a past contract with the waters that they must divide for the Israelites in their time of need. Now their hour of trial is come and they must cross the sea.' It therefore says, "and the sea returned to his former strength.""[161]

The Hebrew word "leaithano" (his strength) also suggests "letano," or the pact that the sea had with the Lord when he created the universe."[162]

The natural tendency and internal energy intelligence of a stream propels it in constant, uninterrupted, flow. The splitting of the Red Sea required the energy intelligence of the seas to remain in suspended animation for the time that was required for the Israelites to cross the Red Sea. In the same fashion, the Lord, at the time of Joshua's need at Beth-Horon, implemented this startling cosmic disruption of the natural function of the cosmos which, by the metaphysical DNA, dictates that the Sun and Moon move along their precise, predistined paths. At the moment when Moses commanded the Red Sea to part, the seas of the *entire world* obeyed His command,[163] changing their internal DNA according to the computerized program inserted by the Lord from the time of their creation.

The story certainly is beyond the belief of even the most pious in today's world. We all have experienced the solar year, consisting of 365 days, during which the Moon circles the Earth and the Earth rotates around the Sun. So, the Sun and Moon should come to a complete standstill simply is an incomprehensible cosmic event, unless we can face the realization that celestial intelligences, otherwise known as celestial internal cosmic energy forces, can be and are directed by man in his altered state of consciousness. If this sort of revolutionary thinking is acceptable, then we can proceed to investigate and ultimately understand how the earth was forced out of its regular motion.

The question is how, where and when did cosmic domination occur that can lead us to believe that Joshua's miracle with the Sun was more than a fascinating fable connected in the mists of time? The key is found in Exodus:[164] "This month shall be unto you the beginning of months. It shall be the first month of the year to you." This is the Bible's first mention of the Zodiac sign Aries as the Rosh Hadashim, the first, or head, of all the months, and the head of the Zodiac system.

The key words in the Exodus verse just quoted are "to you." With that phrase, cosmic control shifted, at the time of Exodus, leaving the children of Israel and with them, all mankind, in control. Without that control, the commandments later handed to Moses on Mount Sinai—"Thou shalt not kill; Thou shalt not steal"—would have been beyond the grasp of a species that always had killed and stolen as naturally as it had breathed. By shifting control to "you," or mankind, the Creator conferred upon his creation an ethic and a responsibility by which he would be bound from that day forth.

With control of the negative cosmic energy by which men had killed and stolen in unconcerned manifestation of their desire to receive for the self alone, they suddenly were able to control and rule themselves. With the fall of Egypt's Middle Kingdom, mankind could tap the positive energy and Aries became the first of all the months, thus bringing all celestial bodies under the domination of man. Joshua, knowing that, literally was able to halt the rotation of the Earth in apparent defiance of all "natural" law.

The month of Exodus, which occurred in Abib, the spring, becomes the first month of the year. Consequently, a strange celestial event was created, dictating that from the moment of the Exodus onward, new cosmic dimensions and forces came into being. With the end of the Middle Kingdom in Egypt, when the great Exodus took place, a new age of cosmology was ushered in.

Before attempting to decodify the significance of Aries as the first sign of the Zodiac, however, let us explore another aspect of this verse. According to Nahmanides,[165] this inauguration of Nissan

(Aries) as the first of the months of the year, was the first commandment ordained upon Israel as a nation. Are we to presume that this
precept, the sanctification of the new moon, was of such importance
that there seemed to be an urgency in proclaiming this commandment while the Jews were yet in Egypt, rather than merely to include
it within the framework of the main commandments of the Torah,
which was promulgated in the wilderness on Mount Sinai? What is
the significance of this precept that was ordained even before the
children of Israel witnessed the declaration of "I am the Lord,"[166] or
the highly moral and ethical doctrines of "Thou shalt not murder;
Thou shalt not steal"? Another point which must be raised in our investigation of this verse, is the fact that this abstruse precept preceded
the final plague, the slaying of the first-born.[168] What hidden cosmic
secret lies in the precept's position among the plagues?

In this connection, a striking observation should be made so far as
conventional astrology is concerned. Conventional astrology clearly
began when man began to observe the heavens. He was very excited
by the moving bodies of the observable solar system against their
starry background. He noted that some of the paths these planets took
somehow seemed to be related to his own situation and background.

Thus, from a conventional astrological viewpoint, man developed
a systematic pattern of celestial events which appeared to have direct
parallels with the affairs of Earth: the obvious connection between the
Moon and the tides, red Mars as the bringer of war, beautiful blue
Venus as the symbol of love and harmony. All conventional astrology
originated when man began to observe the Heavens. Under the
system of astrology originated through Abraham, however, and certainly from the point of view of the new age of physics, what we see in
the Heavens, even with the most powerful of telescopes, might not
even exist. The field of conventional astrology always has been a
wasteland, forever at odds with the scientific world and assuming,
without ever knowing why, that Aries heads the Zodiac, and basing
all the Zodiacal signs upon Greek or Egyptian mythology which has
no place either in Kabbalistic or Biblical views of the subject.

The Zodiac, which is described in the Bible and the Sefer Yetzirah, which preceded the Bible, certainly is a direct contradiction of conventional astrology as to when the signs of the Zodiac were discovered. We obviously do not agree that they were discovered 2,000 years ago, as generally is accepted in scientific circles. Kabbalah contends the Zodiac was discovered about 3,700 years ago. It had always been there, of course — a thin belt of stars stretching across the sky against which the Sun, Moon and planets can be seen to travel. Because all these celestial objects lie near the ecliptic — the plane of the Earth's orbit — the Zodiac is quite narrow, extending only 9 degrees on either side of the ecliptic. Mathematically, the Zodiac is divided into 12 segments, or signs, at 30 degrees of arc. The 12 arcs correspond to the 12 constellations, which are stars that form the actual outlines of the 12 signs.

The fact that the signs are mentioned in the Bible, the Sefer Yetzirah and the Zohar makes Jewish belief in Kabbalistic astrology very evident. For various reasons, however, this has been neglected, with the cosequence that astrology and knowledge of the Zodiac were attributed to the Babylonians, the Greeks and the Egyptians. History has completely omitted the aspect of Kabbalistic astrology.

The rhythm of the Moon, from a Kabbalistic, cosmological, viewpoint, is of such importance that the coming of every month is specifically celebrated. The "celebration," in this case,[169] is not used in a conventional manner, which implies an observance by rote with little or no knowledge of its reason or origin. Inasmuch as we know that what we are discussing are the cosmological effects of each sign of the Zodiac, we shortly will understand, that we're dealing with the tapping of cosmic energies, and what has been provided for us through any form of traditional celebration really is a sophisticated procedure — an intricate and precise method by which we can tap these particular energies for our benefit.

On the Shabbat before each Rosh Hodesh (new moon), the *day* of Rosh Hodesh is announced with a special, unique, service during the Sabbath service and there are prayers by the congregation asking the Lord to make the new month one of life, one of blessing, one of joy and peace. The mystics and Kabbalists of Safed in the 16th century treated the day *before* Rosh Hodesh the same way, fasting and regarding the eve of the new month as a small Yom Kippur or Day of Atonement.[170] Thus, on the day preceding the first day of the lunar month, all Kabbalists would make a pilgrimage to a particular spiritual teacher. In fact, this is a common modern tradition the purpose of which is to connect with the new cosmic energy which shortly will appear.

On the day preceding a new month, and also on the 15th day of that month, we, at the Research Centre in Israel make pilgrimages, or mystical tours, to specific, righteous people, We ask their extraterrestrial intervention to provide us with the opportunity to tap the positive cosmic energy that necessarily will flow during that particular month and to prevent the negative cosmic energies from flowing from under that sign of the Zodiac. We ask to be provided with the means of preventing their negative influences from reaching us and thus becoming manifest in our mundane affairs.

The day of the new moon, itself, is considered a minor festival, and again, "festival" is just another definition of a cosmic event by which prayers have been established. Prayers, for us, are channels by which we can tap the cosmic energy that appears on that particular day. All such holidays and festivals are merely time frames because the naked eye certainly never will observe astrological and cosmological influences stemmming from them. Consequently, what has been provided for in that mass of words called the Bible is merely the timetable of what cosmological events are taking place, when they are taking place and what forces they bring to hand. They are referred to as festivals, or, in the Bible, precepts, by which we can tap that incredible cosmic energy force for our use and prevent negative astral energies from reaching us. Nearly all who "pray" in good faith, whether Jew, Moslem or Christian, will testify that their prayers frequently are answered, but few, if any of them know why. How much more powerful their prayers would be if they did.

After Rosh Hodesh, seven days after the event of the new moon, there is another "traditional" ceremony for the Kidush Livanah, or sanctification of the new moon. This actually was the first "commandment" to the Jews in Egypt, preceding the ten of Judeo-Christian bedrock. It dealt with the first tapping of the positive cosmic energy which alone could offset the power of the Egyptians who knew how to tap the Moon's negative energy. Moses proclaimed the first tapping as necessary to make manifest the 10th plague of Exodus, the slaying of the first-born, in which the Israelites made use of the lamb. In modern parlance, the lamb was the software by which the program of a world totally consumed with negativity could be erased. The Exodus was not for Jews only. All who were enslaved became free on that day and since the lamb was the software of the process, it is easy to see why Aries is the first of months, yet, over thousands of years, no attempt has ever been made by conventional astrology to explain the phenomenon. This remains one of the underlying causes of the dichotomy that stands between the science of astronomy and astrology. Astronomers offer no answers at all. They are content, in their lack of understanding, simply to dispute the validity of astrology which they write off as a mere myth with no real physical affect. Neither the five senses nor conventional science can grasp the unseen internal forces,and what science cannot put in a test tube or under a microscope, science cannot believe.

To further stress the importance of freeing astrology from its prison of mythology and place it in its proper position in science, we must turn to Rabbi Isaac Luria,[171] in discusing the importance of this precept called sanctification of the new moon, says, "This precept of the sanctification of the new moon would now begin with the month of Nissan inasmuch as this month will now be considered the first month." This first month falls during Abib, or spring." Another coded message in Exodus substantiates the importance of the particular season:

"And Moses said unto the people, "Remember this day in which you come out from Egypt, out of the house of bondage, where, by strength of hand, the Lord brought you out from this place. There shall be no leavened bread eaten. This day you go forth in the month of Abib.' "[172]

This particular chapter therefore is contained in our daily prayers, and as Rashi,[173] a commentator on the Bible, declares, we learn from this particular passage that it is a daily obligation[174] of the Jew to recall the Exodus in his daily prayers. The word "meditation" might be substituted for "prayer" in this case since it is by means of meditation that we make use each day of cables that free us from linear time and project us into that consciousness in which there is no time, space or motion. This, effectively, makes time travel a tool which is most effective on the 15th day of Nissan, which is brought about by a conjunction of the solar/lunar months. Only in that month can freedom be proclaimed. Slavery is a condition under which one is subjected to the astral, physical and external energy forces of out planet and of our universe and to man's desire to receive for himself alone.

That is why, in Exodus, it is stressed that "This day you go forth in the month of Abib." This is why the Jew is freed from bondage. The conjunction of the solar aspect of Nissan, Aries and the lunar cycle constitutes a team of incredible energy forces working to produce a celestial confrontation at the time of Exodus. It was a confrontation in which the Jews created a cosmic energy force called freedom, but even today, one cannot have it simply by wishing. The contemporary student of Kabbalah has the same power at his fingertips, but to grasp it, he must apply discipline and meditation. Tradition alone simply will not get the job done. Tradition is little more than the owner's manual spelling out how connections must be made and buttons pushed.

It should be obvious now that dependence solely upon the solar calendar, as in the case of conventional astrology, or upon the lunar year, as Moslems do in pursuit of the art, effectively short-circuits any application of Kabbalistic astrology. Only under the Jewish lunar/solar system can the 15th day of Nissan coincide with or be in conjunction with the Aries aspect of the solar system. Without that, we would miss that particular vital combination of celestial forces under which the required variety of cosmic forces pervades the universe. The method of connection was disclosed in the form of the precept of Kiddush Ha'Hodesh to enable the Jew, at the point of Exodus, to control his entire destiny and not be governed by the ensuing 11 months of negative astral influence.

This, then, is the importance of that particular "day" mentioned in Exodus and we can understand why its proclamation became the first precept. Knowledge is connection and, as indicated earlier, Genesis spells out the synonymous relationship between knowing and connection: "Adam *knew* Eve, his wife, and she conceived and bore Cain."[175] This goes beyond the mere biological coupling by which mammals reproduce their kind. In the case of Adam and Eve, it might be compared with two people who know the same thing about sports, fashion, physics or the weather. When they know, they somehow seem to have a greater affinity. Both are connected to the same thing. Consequently, when we *know* of astrology, when we understand cosmic consciousness and its internal intelligence, then alone we are tuned into the proper channel. That is why Kabbalistic astrology goes to such great lengths to provide knowledge of cosmic energy rather than merely of the natal chart. We are primarily concerned with *knowing*, and when we know the internal and external aspects of cosmic energy, we then are in a position to connect. When we are in a position to connect, then we have the precept of Passover given at this particular time.

The most distressing aspect of what was occurring in Egypt and throughout the world during the time of Israel's bondage was not so much the gravity of all the suffering through which the Jews had been going, but the dampening of the human spirit—the freedom of thought and action so vital to independant individuals. Passover was able to cope with that particular problem and provide freedom to the spirit.

We hear so much today about how the problems raised by technological advances probably are insoluble because they are so numerous and profound. Most people harbor feelings of hopelessness which have almost no precedent in civilization. With the disturbing technological and environmental crisis which seem to crop up almost daily, I am inclined to believe that we will remain on the brink of catastrophe as long as we cannot free ourselves from the problem of not being free, but of being computerized and losing all initiative in the process. Small wonder that so many people believe that our form of technological civilization eventually must collapse if present trends continue.

Today, as never before, we are ruled by an unprecedented inter-connectedness of effects. Something that happens in China directly influences American perceptions and living patterns. Political conflicts in the Middle East seriously affect the world economy. Tyranny in South Africa reverberates on Wall Street. This growing interrelationship has frustrated the attempts of poorer nations to develop effective industries or manage their economies and the frustration has spawned terrorism. With speculations of what still might come — nuclear war, a polluted environment, damage to the ozone layer, acid rain — fear, gloom and hardship prevail, but their whole chorus is nothing more than a replay of history.

It is the Great Exodus, on stage for yet another encore, and the metaphysical connections, by which the Jews dealt with the first one, are still in place and functional for all who have the will and the knowledge to use them.

10

Biblical Space Travel

Space, the final frontier.
These are the voyages of the Star Ship Enterprise.
Its five-year mission: To explore strange new worlds;
To seek out new life and new civilizations;
To boldly go where no man has gone before.

— Star Trek

FOR ALL ITS FUTURISTIC SETTING, THERE WAS NOTHING NEW ABOUT "Star Trek," the now classical television adventure series in which Captain Kirk and his intrepid crew hurtled at "Warp-Nine" across the cosmos, nurturing good, battling evil and looking with awe upon life forms and intelligences never dreamed of on Earth. What the Star Ship Enterprise did for five fictional years, Kabbalists have been doing factually for centuries, and they needed no technological hardware to accomplish their mission.

The Torah is filled with references to what can only be called space transportation systems. The purpose of this book is not merely to recount them, but to propose how man now effectively can make use of this information in order to delve more deeply into the mysteries of our universe and understand the control such mysteries exercise over his cosmic destiny. It proposes that those who can ascend to a higher, or altered, state of consciousness can become welded into the outer space connection, and that conventional religion should not picture itself as a static, dogmatic community, but rather as a channel by which such higher consciousness can be achieved.

The Bible's recorded events are merely coded presentations of more intelligent and higher forms of extraterrestrial life which can assist such lower forms as we by causing changes for the better in our metaphysical DNA. Before the fall, Adam could communicate with extraterrestrial levels of unsurpassed intelligence in cosmic energy fields. Denied that ability by the advent of sin, which is to say, our insatiable desire to receive for the self alone, we now struggle back toward that lost plateau of Eden, still hungry "to boldly go where no man has gone before." We are in the process of planning and testing space machines for interplanetary travel, but the most sanguine of scientists give little hope that we ever will be able to replicate the Star Ship Enterprise and extend our physical sphere to the stars. They are so far away that even at "Warp One"—the speed of light aboard the Enterprise—most of them would not be accessible in a lifetime. They are not, however, inaccessible to the Kabbalist, as is evidenced by descriptions of "space vehicles" in the Zohar and the Torah. Let us browse among available models.

One of the first accounts of such a vehicle was revealed when Moses and the Israelites were traveling from Egypt ot the Promised Land. They were accompanied on their trek across the wilderness by a space ship that looked like a pillar of cloud: "And the Lord went before them by day in a pillar of cloud to lead them the way, and by night in a pillar of fire."[176] The Zohar, exploring the implications of this peculiar passage, explains it as follows:[177] "The expression, 'and the Lord,' means the all-inclusive intelligence energy force and His Council."

"This illustrates what we have been taught," said R. Isaac, "Namely that the Patriarchs were the Shekinah's chariot. Abraham is indicated by the words "walked before them by day;" (the aspect of the positive, right-column magnetic energy force) Isaac by "in a pillar of cloud;" (the aspect of the negative, left-column magnetic energy force) Jacob by "to lead them the way;" (the aspect of the neutral, central- column magnetic energy force) and David by the words, "by night in a pillar of fire" (the aspect of all three forces unified and now manifested). All these four formed the supernal chariot for the assistance and guardianship of Israel, to the end that she might walk in harmony, completeness and peace." The Biblical description of the vehicle is set forth in terms by which space transportation could be understood in those days—a chariot.

That higher forms of life intelligence existed long before the Great Exodus is well established in the Zohar,[178] particularly at the time of the tower of Babel: We read, "Blessed be the name of God from everlasting to everlasting; for wisdom and might are his."[179] Whenever the Lord permitted the deep mysteries of wisdom to be brought down into the world, mankind was corrupted by them. He gave supernal wisdom to Adam, but Adam utilized the wisdom to familiarize himself with the negative grades as well until, in the end, he attached himself to the evil side and the fountains of wisdom were closed to him. After he repented before the Lord, parts of the wisdom again were revealed to him in the book given to him by the Angel Raziel. But through that same knowledge, his descendants again abused it. Adam gave this book of wisdom to Noah, who indeed benefitted mankind with its knowledge, but, like all the rest, he later abused it as well. Thus we see that by virture of fragments retained later on, people built a tower of hubris and did various kinds of mischief until their language was confounded and they were scattered over the face of the Earth, bereft of wisdom or purpose.

In the age of Aquarius, however, the Lord again will cause wisdom to be disseminated throughout the world and the people will worship Him, as it is written: "And I will set my spirit within you."[180] In contrast with generations of old, who used it for the ruin of their world, the verse continues in reassurance for those to come: "I will cause you to walk in my statutes and you shall keep mine ordinances and do them."[181]

But the vehicles so graphically described in Exodus are not the only ones in which the patriarchs were able to move through the cosmos. Witness this one: "And the living creatures ran and returned as the appearance of a flash of lightning."[182]

Ezekiel was, first of all, the outstanding prophet during the Babylonnian exile. He was exceptional and unique among the Hebrew prophets as the only prophet whose sphere of activity lay outside the Land of Israel. However, this was not the only exceptional characteristic of Ezekiel's prophetic career. He was unique both in the nature of his vision and in his mode of expression.

The most remarkable section of the Book of Ezekiel is the opening chapter. Here, the prophet describes his personal experience with the Divine Chariot. This gave rise to a system of esoteric thought known in Kabbalistic literature as Ma'aseh Merkabah, the speculation of the Divine Chariot. This branch of esoteric teaching dealt with the natural sciences and Merkabah metaphysics.

While in accordance with the teaching of the Talmud,[183] the account of the creation is not to be expounded in the presence of more than one person and the story of the Merkabah not even to one unless he be wise. Nevertheless, the less important parts of the Merkabah may be taught to those of high moral standard and perfection.

Support for this permission may be found in the Jewish daily morning prayers in the liturgy of the Festivals. The famous Merkabah hymn, Ha'adereth ve'emunah le'hai olamim, referred to as the sons of the angels, is recited by many congregations every Shabbat in the morning ritual and in all synagogues on the Day of Atonement. Above all, the first chapter of the Book of Ezekiel is the selection for the haftorah on the first day of the Feast of Pentecost, a fitting theme for the anniversary of the revelation on Mount Sinai.

The significance of the Patriarchs as chariots of varied energy intelligence has been discussed at length in "Kabbalah for the Layman".[184] "The Patriarchs are the Merkabah," declares the Midrash.[185] Ezekiel's vision suggests that the soul of man—any man—is endowed with the capability of acting as a chariot. Ezekiel's Ophannim Hoyoth[186] and Galgallim (wheels, living creatures and wheel work) form the Divine Chariot in outer space. So, too, were the

Patriarchs the Divine Chariots on the terrestrial level. Ezekiel's vision brought the Glory of the Lord down to the mundane sphere. The Glory of the Lord, in Kabbalistic terminology, is the force or energy source of the Lord, and to bring it down to the terrestrial is to connect and control the Divine Chariot.

Let us pause for a moment to explore some of the phenomena that we have witnessed in our own time and in our own mode of expression. Practically every scientific invention of the 20th century has been predicted in a science fiction story. Who does not remember the formidable Buck Rogers when he first wielded his ray gun in "Armageddon 2419 A.D.," or H.G. Well's "War of the Worlds" in which aliens wrought destruction on the Earth with an invisible heat ray? It was exciting stuff, and except for the extraterrestrial aliens from other planets, much of it either is, or soon will be, science fact.

Science fiction deals with change. Scientists today realize that science fiction is a window of the future. Human-powered flight aircraft, once thought of as impossible, are on the drawing boards. If we come to the realization that the mind supercedes and surpasses physical energy, then how far are we from mind-powered aircraft?

This is precisely the vision to which Ezekiel was referring. To the Kabbalist, metaphysics is learning the rules of a beautiful game that consists of the natural laws and principles of the universe. Those rules, unfortunately, are not well understood and are in the domain of a select few. Most of the time, science plays the game at a much lower level and confusion reigns. To work at the level of root and origin is very rare.

Many years ago, social worker Betty Hill and her husband claimed to have been abducted by short, bald-headed aliens who took them aboard a UFO where they were subjected to medical examination. The tale catapulted the Hills into the tenuous role of celebrated UFO contactees. Large numbers of people believe in the existence of UFOs and believe them to be manned by extraterrestrial visitors. For the present, the UFO story is science fiction. For the Bible, however, the Age of Aquarius is the dawning of space travel as Ezekiel knew it when he described his "space ship."

"And their appearance and their work was, as it were, a wheel within a wheel...and when the living creatures went, the wheels went hard by them; and when the living creatures were lifted up from the bottom, the wheels were lifted up."

The quoted passage is a clear reference to space vehicles and the extraterrestrial aliens that manned them. The Zohar[188] interprets the vision of Ezekiel in the following manner:

"And the living creatures ran and returned as the appearance of a flash of lightning. The concealed lights were revealed and although revealed, the energy intelligences of concealment remained as before, At times they appear, and at other times, they remain concealed. At times, they appear as one color and then at other times, another color. Sometimes, the energy intelligence of one of the Names of the Lord is used, and immediately another craft appears with another Name of the Lord. No one can tolerate or remain fast in its presence."

This is the secret meaning of the above-mentioned verse, "as they depart and appear in a flash." So, too, for the observer, they appear, depart and appear again within one's own intelligence, unlike the prophets who observe the lower terrestrial level and comprehend the upper level connecting with cosmic consciousness of the celestial level, the Metatron Angel. The Metatron Angel rules over and controls a fleet of 4,500 squadrons and its 45 million energy light intelligences.

Each time the fleet departs or enters, 1,500 galaxies tremble and vibrate. A flaming fire follows Metatron's departure from and re-entry to her base. Within this fiery flame are engraved the various letters of the "Shem Ha'Meforish," the secret of the mystical names that control and direct extraterrestrial activity."

Is anybody out there? The Zohar seems to think so. We are indeed not alone in the universe, though there are no others extant in humankind's corporeal form — nor are there any who are independent of human activity.

It is at once exciting and frightening for a world that, only a short while back, thought of itself as both the spiritual and physical center of cosmos. The Zohar maintains that humankind controls and diverts extraterrestrial activity, so, still in keeping with the foresight of science fiction, how does one respond to an extraterrestrial, alien invasion? Will humankind be at the mercy of the aliens? According to the Zohar, spiritually advanced aliens travel in the form of pure intelligent energy that moves faster than the speed of light. Does this necessarily spell the doom of our universe? Are we really helpless in the event of attack where the undamaged victor could dictate terms to a disarmed and helpless loser?

The earth in upheaval has been recorded in the Books of Prophets, stating, "The Earth trembled and the Heavens dropped. . . the mountains melted."[189] King David recorded a similar calamity when he wrote, "The Earth shook, the Heavens also dropped at the presence of the energy intelligence of Elohim; even Sinai itself was moved."[190]

What seems to emerge from the preceding verses is that Deborah and King David appear to have been unaffected by the calamity they, themselves, recorded. How?

"Now as I behold the living creatures, behold one wheel upon the Earth by the living creatures with his four faces."[191] The wheel actually is the consciousness level of neshama (soul), although the Hebrew word of a (wheel) usually indicates the consciousness level of nefesh (crude spirit). The reason for this is to reveal the steps in the cosmic connection with extraterrestrial spacecraft. When the crude spirit has become elevated to the consciousness level of soul, then the connection has been completed and the "space craft" is at hand. . . . [192]

It is an admitted premise that we cannot know the truth about the origin of the planetary systems which came into being billions of years ago. In fact, the problem of the origin and evolution of the solar system suffers from the label, speculation. It is frequently said that most, if not all, postulated theories by scientists wind up with a "but we cannot be certain" comment at the end. It is, I believe, only common sense that prompts us to raise the question, "if we were not there when it all started, then how can we legitimately arrive at any conclusion as to how it was formed?"

The Zohar, therefore, is a refreshing relief for those lost in the maze of computer printouts on matters of the cosmos. The Zohar describes the primeval chaos and just about everything there is to know about our universe.

Contacts between celestial bodies are not limited to the celestial bodies themselves. In this book, containing the cosmic connection between man and cosmos, I have endeavored to show that man determines the activity of our solar system. The reason that cosmic catastrophe occurs so infrequently in historical time is precisely due to human activity which has undergone very little change. Still, change has occurred more than once without conclusive explanation.

Without the Kabbalah, the stories of catastrophe as they can be reconstructed from the records of man and nature, never can be complete. The Zohar provides the missing bits of information that we can employ in a better understanding of the nature of man and his cosmic environment.

The development of the Jewish religion comes under a new light and dimension. The facts presented on Mount Sinai never made an attempt to establish religion as a mode of behavior. Rather, they were established to help humankind trace the origin and evolution of our universe, understand the relationship between cosmos and man and, more importantly, man's purpose within the complexity of it all.

One may ask why, if there are so many civilizations in the universe, none ever has communicated with us? "Because," states the Zohar, "One must achieve a level of consciousness and awareness for contact with intelligent life in the universe."[193] Earth's radio presence, a mere 50 years old, is not the route in our determination to establish contact and constitutes, at best, a worthless exercise.

The universe is teeming with life — intelligent thought life — amid the hundreds of billions of stars that stud the galaxies. Why can we not have Ezekiel's vision to witness it all?

Again, the Zohar provides an answer: "Said Rabbi Shimon, 'Alas for the blindness of the sons of men, all unaware as they are how full the Earth is of strange and invisible beings and hidden dangers. Could they see, they would marvel how they, themselves, can exist on Earth.'"[194]

Our search in determining man's place in the cosmos thus is only half the task. The other is to establish the sort of power and influence man has on his environment, terrestrial and extraterrestrial, and understand the power nature holds over us. The space ships of Ezekiel and Exodus are at our fingertips if only we can rise to the occasion by elevating our souls to that state of consciousness in which they can be utilized. The Starship Enterprise, in all its journeys, never faced so sublime an adventure.

11

Human Star Wars

The end-all of knowledge is to know that we cannot know everything. But there are two sorts of not-knowing. The one is when a man does not begin to examine and try to know because it is impossible to know. The other examines and seeks until he comes to know that one cannot know everything.

— Baal Shem-Tov

IT IS SELF-APPARENT THAT WE FIND OURSELVES IN A STATE OF WORLD-wide crisis and for the very first time, we have come face to face with an awesome reality of the possible extinction of the entire human race and all forms of life on our planet. Nevertheless, the resounding words of the prophet Ezekiel provide some hope for the future and welcome alternative to the threat of a nuclear catastrophe. With the new astronomical discoveries of the 70's, we have been brought face to face with a phenomenon more outlandish and more bizarre than any encountered ever before in the history of science; the catostraphic gravitational collapse which predictably results in a Black Hole or nak-ed singularity. Being an utterly lawless entity, a singularity should cause totally chaotic and random influences. It is to this very chaotic possibility that the prophet addresses himself. The Jews, through whom the energy-intelligence program system was revealed in coded

form on Mt. Sinai and subsequently decodified through the Sefer
Yetzirah and Zohar, were provided with given detailed laws and in-
struction by the Tetragrammaton through Moses and R. Shimon Bar
Yohai. This did not necessitate any clairvoyant powers, but rather
the knowledge that would permit a connection with space vehicle
systems channeled by intellligence energy. This is what I refer to as
the outer space connection[195] space vehicle. To which Adam, before
the sin, had been connected. He ate (connected) of the Tree of Life
and lived forever until he decided to take the lower universal life
course of "good and evil." "And the Lord formed man of the dust of
the ground and breathed into his nostrils the breath of life; and man
became a living soul."[196] The Zohar[197] provides the following interpretation of this verse: "The breath of life was enclosed in the Earth,
which was made pregnant with it like a female impregnated by the
male. So the dust and the breath were joined, and the dust became
full of spirits and souls." When the Lord breathed into Adam the
breath of life and he became a living creature, the words 'into his
nostrils' unveils the mystery of the entire verse and the secret of life
itself. The code word "nostrils" reflects the cosmic energy intelligence
of *"Ze'ir Anpin"* the outer space connection.[198] Life, which is cell divi-
sion, is caused by Ze'ir Anpin in as much as all living entities human,
animal or plant, are composed at the time of death of exactly the same
physical material before and after death. The difference is that in life,
cells divide, chemical reactions exist and molecules change, whereas
in death, cells do not divide. Such is the energy intelligence force in
the mystery creation of *all* things in the universe. The connection is
the Tetragrammaton, the channels are the laws and principles of the
Bible.

"This is the book of generations of Adam. In the day that the Lord
created man, in the likeness of the Lord made he him."[199] Following
the Zoharic tradition of unlocking the mysteries surrounding the
tremendous supply of stored intelligence and knowledge contained in
the invisible, universal brain bank, we find a decodifying expression
of the verse quoted above. "R. Abba said: "The Lord did indeed send
down a book to Adam, from which he became acquainted with the
supernal wisdom. It came later into the hands of the "sons of the

Lord," the wise of their generation, and whoever was privileged to pursue it could learn from it supernal wisdom. This book was brought down to Adam by the "master of mysteries," preceded by three messengers. When Adam was expelled from the Garden of Eden, he tried to keep hold of the book, but it flew out of his hands. He then pleaded with the Lord with tears for its return, and it was given back to him, in order that wisdom might not be forgotten of men, and that they might strive to obtain knowledge of their Master. Tradition further tells us that Enoch also had a book, which came from the same place as the book of the generations of Adam. When the Lord took him, he showed him all supernal mysteries and the Tree of Life in the midst of the Garden and its leaves and branches, all of which can be found in his book."

The intelligence, knowledge, energy and its manifested physical laws of expression always have been in existence as they are now. Looking backward in time, there was no less total universal intelligence at an earlier time than is now recognized in our day. The cosmic life cycles of our universe, which appear as a continuous expanding cosmology experience, changes in a *physical* evolutionary process. The energy-intelligence itself remains above space-time principles.

Where, then, is this book for peoples living in the age of Aquarius referred to by the prophet Ezekiel as previously mentioned? Where is this knowledge for humankind that may provide the intelligence-energy to mentally control and direct the motion and circumstances of the whole of our universe? What, if any, cosmic bonds already exist that may unite our universe and its inhabitants with the heavens above which contain the potential of all mass and all time? After all, has any segment of the scientific community created something that had no prior existence? Even beginnings or ends of terrestrial entities are merely changes in the cycles of our universe or results of other cosmic changes which have profound and sometimes irreversible effects on each other? Because of the essential limitations of the rational mind, we have to accept the fact that scientific ideas and theories have limited range in its description of reality. When science extended the range of their particular probing into the unfamiliar subatomic realm of reality, they were confronted with the realization that most of their fundamental frames of reference were in need of revision. They could no longer deal with approximate and limited views of universal reality. So while our society urgently needs changes in our attitudes towards achieving a deeper understanding of the world around us, our value system requires careful reexamination which must, of necessity, bring about far-reaching changes in our society. The ultimate question still remaining for us to grapple with is where is this body of knowledge, if it does in fact exist, that we may draw from to meet and achieve our objective of turning ultimate destruction to everlasting and eternal peace and tranquility?

"In your compendium, R. Shimon Bar Yohai, The Book of Splendor, The Zohar, shall Israel in the future taste from the Tree of Life which is the Book of Splendor, and the world shall go forth from its exile with mercy."[201]

The future is here and now. The Kabbalah connection awaits us all for those who merely extend a welcome hand.

"R. Hiya said, "In the days of R. Shimon Bar Yohai even the birds utter wisdom, for his words are known above and below.' R. Hiya then quoted the verse, "And the Lord said to Moses, Behold thou shalt sleep with thy fathers."[202] 'Mark this,' he said, "As long as Moses was alive, he used to check Israel from sinning. And because Moses was among them, there shall not be a generation like that one till the days of the Messiah. How much more those who stand before R. Shimon and learn from him, and how very much more R. Shimon himself, who is above all! Alas for the world when R. Shimon shall depart, and the fountains of wisdom shall be closed, and men shall seek wisdom and there will be none to impart it, and the Torah will be interpreted erroneously because there will be none who is acquainted with wisdom! Said R. Judah: The Lord will one day reveal the hidden mysteries of the Torah, namely, at the time of the Messiah, because 'the Earth shall be full of the knowledge of the Lord like the waters cover the sea'[203] and as it is written 'They shall teach *no more* every man his neighbor or every man his brother, saying, Know the

Lord (Tetragrammaton), for they shall all know me from the smallest
to the greatest of them.'"[204]

Many of the challenging topics discussed in science today, especially the nature of Black Holes, the consequences of gravitational collapse, early stages of the Big Bang, present science with a crisis un-
paralleled in history. Progress in science had become so commonplace
that most people have accepted it as a natural process of the interpretation of nature. For centuries now, we have assumed that
however abstruse an aspect of nature may have appeared, science
would always find the answer. Recently, and only in the past few
decades, has the scientific community come to the realization that we
are faced with a bewildering and confusing array of complex life
forms and fail to adequately cope with the new physics. On the other
hand, the deeper our probing, the simpler the task will become and
we shall appear on the threshold of a whole new era of physics.

The route to the new physics of the future lies beyond the dimension of physical reality of our world. It will permit us to go beyond
spacetime in our analysis, and hopefully, one day a door will open, no
wider than the eye of a needle, and unto us shall open the supernal
gates exposing the glittering interrelatedness of the universe with all
its beauty and simplicity.[205] Towards the arrival of that date, the
Zohar holds out more hope than a science that must rely largely on
randomness and probability. The Book of Splendor intends to provide a direct link and contact with the universal energy-intelligence
that we discussed previously and subsequently present the world of
metaphysics as an exact, simplified science. The new science of the
Kabbalah does indeed answer many of the enigmatic aspects of
nature, yet still it remains elegantly simple. The new physics of Kabbalah and Einsteinian classical physics may be brought into agree-
ment by a better understanding of what each represent in their
respective frames of reference. The Zohar's world view of our
universe transcends and occupies a frame beyond space-time, wheras
the modern new age of physics remains fixed and limited to the
frames as presented by Einstein.

The new Kabbalistic vision of reality that we have been talking
about is based on an indepth perception of the Bible's coded narra-

tions and tales. The description provided by the Bible sounds quite similar to the description of modern space systems. It emphasizes the outer space connection as the energy-intelligent system referred to as the Tree of Life.

"And Moses was one hundred and twenty years."[206] "This is an allusion to Moses," states the Zohar,[207] through whose agency the Law was given and who bestowed life on men from the Tree of Life. And in truth had Israel not sinned with the Golden Calf, they would have been proof against death, since the Tree of Life had been brought *down* to them. Hence we have learnt, Moses did *not* die, but he was *gathered* in from this world and caused the Moon to shine, being in this respect like the Sun, which also after setting does not expire but gives light to the Moon.

R. Elazar said: The Lord will one day *re-establish* the world and strengthen the spirit of the sons of men so that they may prolong their days *forever*, as it is written, "For as the days of a tree so shall be the days of my people, etc."[208]

Did Moses die? Is he actually still alive? When Moses was 120 years old he was told by the Lord to go up unto the mountains of Moab, "and the Lord buried him in the Land of Moab, but no *man* knoweth of his sepulchre unto this day."[209] Is it conceivable that his body did not remain on Earth but was transported (*gathered*) by a space vehicle to outer space (*heaven*)? The Zohar states, incredible as it may seem, that Moses did *not* die. His cosmic bond with the outer space connection, the Tree of Life, was never severed as was the case with the Israelites after the Golden Calf incident. Had the Israelites not sinned, their cosmic connection with the Tree of Life would have eternally remained, and their days on earth "prolonged forever," states the Zohar. What is the significance of the Zoharic comparison of Moses to the Sun?

Like everyone else, I have been curious enough to ask is there really extraterrestrial life on other planets or elsewhere. As an increasing number of scientists search for evidence of extraterrestrial intelligence, or if they ever visited Earth on some kind or transport system, the more I am slowly coming to the conclusion that the answer may rest with a possibility that has already been alluded to both in the Bible and the Zohar. Preposterous as it may sound, and despite the lack of hard evidence to support the existence of extraterrestrial life, a number of scientists are becoming increasingly vocal about its possibility, *not to mention* the popular recognition and acceptability despite the statistical evidence against it.

Before proceding to explore and interpret the Zoharic account of the death of Moses, I would like to relate another account of Biblical space transportation, one very similar to the startling pattern recorded in Deuteronomy, which most probably has been overlooked by most of us because of our educational mental programming.

"And Elijah took his mantle, wrapped it together, smote the waters and they were divided, so that they two went over on dry ground. And it came to pass, as they still went on, and talked, that, behold, there appeared a chariot of fire, and horses of fire, and parted them both asunder; and Elijah went up by a whirlwind into heaven. Elisha saw it, and cried,' My father, my father, the chariot of Israel and the horsemen.' And he saw him no more."[210]

The striking similarities between the two Biblical accounts, the two main characters of paranormal phenomena, the possibility of space travel and finally the presentation of eternal life, will hopefully provide a framework for understanding and communication data and as a basis for gaining insight into our universe. It now appears far more complex and bewildering than was suspected a mere two decades ago. It is clear that the present scientific world view of our universe still is in its infancy, but the quest for unification and interrelatedness has become one of the principle areas of investigation in modern physics. Perhaps, explaining all of nature in terms of a single unified energy intelligence will ultimately be realized. Our investigation of Biblical phenomena shall take us along a path of physical laws presently unknown to us, but utilized by Moses and Elijah.

Even a modest attempt to review all of the facets mentioned in these two Biblical accounts would burst the fame of a book much larger than this one. Consequently, I shall address and limit my inquiry to the energy intelligence known as the Tree of Life, space transportation and eternal life which appears in our subject material.

Moses and Elijah were observed leaving Earth. Elisha describes the space transport as a chariot of fire with horses of fire similar to the exhaust of a modern day rocket engine. Moses, states the Zohar, did not die. His body was trasported to Heaven, in similar fashion as that recorded by Elisha. Moses' body was not seen after his death. These two were again seen alive when they appeared before R. Shimon Bar Yohai and his son R. Elazar in the cave of P'quin where the revelation of the Zohar took place.[211] In the seclusion of the cave, R. Simon was visited twice a day by the prophet Elijah, who revealed to him the secrets of the Zohar. The deeper and more comprehensive sections, known as the Ra'ya Mehemna, are a record of the discourses that took place between R. Shimon and Moses himself, the beloved shepherd. These meetings took place hundreds of years after their departure from the Earth. How was this possible and by what means was it accomplished?

The cloud or chariot, their space vehicle transport was continually with them, either for their journey to outer space or their return to Earth. The universal energy intelligent force was making contact with R. Shimon and his son Elazar through extraterrestrial Moses and Elijah. R. Shimon had made contact with the outer space connection, the Tree of Life, to which Adam before the sin had been connected. The connection of Moses and Elijah to the Tree of Life would remain eternal. Consequently, they could not nor would they meet the inevitable finale of all flesh, death. They did not die, but would remain as the Sun, which after setting does not expire but given light to the moon, as portrayed so beautifully by the Zohar.[212] Extraterrestial righteous individuals always have according to the Bible and Zohar, been instrumental in helping humankind on this earth.

"And it came to pass when Joshua was by Jericho, that he lifted up his eyes and looked and there stood a man against him with sword drawn in his hand: Joshua went to him and said to him, Are you for or against us? And he said, Nay; I come before you as captain of the host of the Lord. Joshua fell on his face to the earth and worshipped, saying: What saith my Lord unto his servant? And the captain of the Lords' host said unto Joshua, Remove thy shoe of thy foot; for the place where you are standing is sacred. Joshua did so. And the Lord said unto Joshua, See, I have given into thine hand Jericho, its king and mighty men of valor. Joshua the son of Nun called the priest, and said unto them, take up the ark of the covenant and let seven priests bear seven sounding horns before the ark of the Lord.[213]

The rest is biblical history. "The captain of the host of the Lord, "an extraterrestrial individual came to the assistance of Joshua and the Israelites by providing the system by which a cosmic connection to the energy intelligent force, the Tree of Life, will have been achieved. The ark of the covenant, which played so important a role in Israels' conquest of the Holy Land served as a space station through which the energy intelligent force would become manifest. The loss of the ark in later years spelled doom for the Jews. But for the present the "walls of Jericho came tumbling down" and the rest is history.

This was the same ark of the covenant that had been carried by the Jews during their 40 years of wandering through the wilderness. "Thou shalt put into the ark the testimony, the Torah, which I shall give thee."[214] Instilled with extraterrestrial intelligence by virtue of its eternal cosmic connection to the Tree of Life, this same ark was instrumental in many miraculous, paranormal phenomenal events during the time of King David. "And when they came to Nachon's threshingfloor, Uzzah put forth *his hand* to the ark of the Lord and took hold of it for the oxen shook it. And the anger of the Lord was kindled against Uzzah; and the Lord (the Tetragrammaton) smote him there for his error and he died by the ark of the Lord.[215] The ark contained an incredible degree of cosmic energy force, so powerful that it struck down Uzzah and he died on the spot.

The celestial struggle at the Red Sea was a marvelous spectacle that never has been forgotten. It is mentioned in numerous verses throughout the Bible. It was an unusual event, and because it was so unusual, it has remained as one of the most impressive cosmic upheavals in the long history of the Jewish people.

"And Moses stretched out his hand over the sea; and the Lord caused the sea to go *back* by strong east wind all that night, and made the sea dry land, and the waters were divided.[216] All nations and peoples of the world experienced this enormous cosmic energy intelligence force, that instantly pervaded the entire universe, according to the biblical commentator Rashi. Because of the grammatical structure of this verse, and as explained by the Mehilta, "the waters of all oceans and seas was divided."[217] A unified energy force at work with no beginning or end, itself eternal as the cosmics present and flowing equally without relation to anything external[218] was the cosmic power force tapped by Moses. Moses provided a cosmic connection for the children of Israel that would control the molecular movement of the water forming it into two vertical walls. A cosmic upheaval of such proportions swept through every corner of the Earth and universe, and the traditions of many peoples along with cosmological myth persist that seas were torn apart, "waters were piled up to the height of sixteen hundred miles and they could be seen by all the nations of the world."[219] This peculiar demonstration in which Moses drew the all-inclusive positive cosmic energy force by tapping the source of this energy from the Tree of Life, gives us a futuristic panorama of the new physical laws of nature. Scientists today are discovering a whole array of new phenomena, many of which have taken us from the familiar material world that belongs to human experience to a signpost pointing to a more complex view of reality. Time and space, objectively speaking, have almost vanished in the paranormal, the worlds of metaphysics, along a path strewn with paradoxes and strange phenomena. These Biblical incidents all suggest concepts and things that will hopefully be rediscovered leading eventually to a redefinition of reality in a way that all mankind shall understand and see.

The journey pursued in these pages has been an attempt to track down the cosmic power sources of our universe, and to embark as in all other journeys once the cosmic connection has been bonded, toward unity with the father of our universe, the all embracing unity of energy intelligence.

The applied science of cosmic energy again was demonstrated by Elijah the prophet when he parted the sea. Elijah, having made his connection with the Tree of Life force, intervened in the physical affairs of matter with fantastical phenomena and strange descriptions. The links that do exist between the scientific and the apparently paranormal were presented in Biblical verses as demonstrations that the world around us of unconnected and yet interrelated events is merely a manifestation of an all embracing whole.

The course of the all inclusive positive energy force, the Light of Wisdom to give and provide mankind the knowledge and intelligence to reconcile the finite with the infinite, was therefore left to Moses and Elijah. As extraterrestrial personalities, they were destined to transmit the knowledge and application of the Tree of Life which emerges as the Book of Splendor, the Zohar. Celestial mechanics no longer would conflict with cosmic reality. If the activity in an atom constitutes the paradigm for the physical world, then the Biblical events mentioned in this book are not merely accidents of celestial movement but occurrences as normal as birth and death. Links between the extraterrestrial and our physical universe no longer are limited to the domain of human perception.

Taken all together, the world of metaphysics has become closely aligned with the world of physical reality all around us. Taking this point to its extreme, let us explore the power of mind waves that, within the forseeable future, will become detectable with improved scientific instruments. I refer to a cosmic intelligent force that can be directed at will. As life in space becomes less of an adventure and takes on the trappings of the routine, future wars very well may be waged in space precisely for the reason that the very depth of space will have become as familiar to us as our own backyard, which has and continues to serve as a playground for human suffering and war-torn destruction. Opposing space satellite armadas, like their airborne counterparts of another time, will be trading fire with each other in a zero-dimension confrontation. In anticipation of wars in which enemy planes and satellites will be traveling at speeds faster than the speed of light, high speed computer techniques will be developed which could indicate quickly the most effective response to an enemy threat. Artificial intelligence systems will handle decision making and all that will be left to the defense command is the pushing of a button. The battle should not take more than a few minutes before victor and vanquished are determined. Science fiction? Well, let us explore the first space-star war directed, not by computers, but by actual physical energy signals created by the thought process as a brain wave.

"And Balak the son of Zippor saw all that Israel had done to the Amorites."[220] "What did he see," asks the Zohar.[221] He saw both through the *window* of wisdom and with his physical eyes. There is one window through which the very essence of wisdom can be seen. He was the son of a bird, (Zippor means in Hebrew, bird), for he used birds for all his metaphysical arts. The bird would come to him and tell him certain things. One day, Balak did his usual thing with the bird and it flew away, never to return. He was greatly distressed, and then he saw it coming with a fiery flame following it and burning its wings. This was the thinking process of Moses, generating fiery energy against the Amorites in Heshbon: "For there is a fire gone out of Heshbon, a flame from the city of Sihon: It hath cosumed Ar of Moab, and the Lords of the high places of Arnon."[222] The tapping of this energy by Moses permitted the intelligent energy force, through mental effort, to control the molecular motion of the birds "wing thereby preventing it from flying.[223]

Mind control of this nature was a principle reserved for only a select few kabbalists. However in the age of Aquarius, all mankind shall *know*.[224] The thought process of mind control whereby thought processes may control the movement of molecules has had its use during the episode of the Great Exodus. More specifically this procedure is demonstrated by the Jews during the Passover Seder when he designates the three matzohs as Kohen, Levi, Israel.[225] While for the present, the controlled direction of an atom by our thought processes cannot be scientifically detected, the Sages of the Haggadah suggested the designation of the three matzohs, whereby they provided the Jew with the knowledge and method by which mind power would move the atom as well as the movement of infinite atoms within the matzoh thereby achieving a cosmic connection with the all inclusive positive energy intelligence. This energy intelligence produces for the individual on Passover a personal Exodus from bondage, that freedom from want that so few of us ever experience. The designation of one matzoh, as Kohen by the mind (inasmuch as the matzoh, which was just a few seconds ago in a box together with all other matzohs, now assumes another dimension of cosmology, Kohen) temporarily changes the characteristic of the matzoh, inserting one's own energy force, rearranging the molecules so that the positive, right column force of the atom became the dominant molecule of the matzoh, which is referred to as the Kohen matzoh of positive domination. The same procedure continues for the second matzoh by which the dominant molecule is negative or left column, Levi. Finally, the third matzoh becomes the dominant energy force of the central column, the neutron designated as Israel.[226]

Consequently, if we were to ask of ourselves, will man progress to a sufficiently high level to make use of mind control and thereby make the connection with the Tree of Life, the outer space connection; my answer would be in the affirmative, in as much as this phenomena already has been demonstrated by an entire nation — the Jewish nation during the Great Exodus.

I would be remiss if I closed this chapter without mentioning one of the serious outcomes of our newly established phenomena, of mind and molecular control of matter. With this control, it is very likely that *Homo sapiens* one day will fly without the use of aircraft, spacecraft or any other physical means of transportation. Legend provides us with numerous accounts of flights by Elijah, R. Shimon and R. Isaac Luria, wherby they rose into the air and travelled from Galilee to Jerusalem. This brings us to an account recorded in the Zohar,[227] which I must confess, probably is the most fascinating, incredible yet actual account of human flight through space ever recorded.

"R. Elazar said: "Who killed the wicked Balaam, and how was he killed? R. Isaac replied "Pinhas and his comrades killed him, as it says 'they slew on their slain.'[228] We have learnt that through his magic arts, he and the kings of Midian were able to fly in the air. And it was the Holy Frontlet[229] of the High Priest and the meditation of the Pinhas that brought them down 'on their slain.' Said R. Elazar: 'I know all this.' R. Shimon then said: 'Elazar, Balaam was a powerful adversary, as it says, "There arose not a prophet in Israel like Moses,"'[230] but there did arise among other nations, to wit, Balaam, who was supreme among the lower Crowns (lower frame of reference of intelligent energy, lesser mind control of the atom) as Moses was among the upper Crowns (higher level of intelligent energy control).

How then were they able to kill him? The answer lies in a remark from the Book of Wisdom of King Solomon. The level of intelligent energy mind control is determined by and dependent upon three signs of a mans' character: paleness is a sign of anger, talking is a sign of folly, and self-praise is a sign of ignorance.

It is true that it says, 'Let a stranger praise thee and not thy own mouth,'[231] and we alter this to 'Let a stranger praise thee.' But the wicked Balaam praised himself in everthing, and deceived people as well. He made much of little; consequently, his egocentricity prevented him from achieving a higher altered state of consciousness. For all that he said of himself referred only to the unclean grades. Though it was true, it did not mean much. Though whoever heard it, imagined that he surpassed all the prophets of the world."

When we raised the question as to whether humankind could sufficiently elevate himself or herself to a spiritual level of altered consciousness connecting with the outer space connection, the Tree of Life, and subsequently control by thought or molecular motion in matter which ultimately leads to the ability to fly, the Zohar and the Bible provide factual accounts that mankind can control matter in the same manner that we control external mind control over parts of our bodies. The possibility of man achieving flying ability without the use of physical means of transportation already had existed when humankind progressed to the level of cosmic connection to the Tree of Life, the link to the outer space connection. Using and abusing such powers selfishly, as did Balaam, was accompanied by a decline and ultimate disintegration and general loss of harmony among *Homo sapiens* which inevitably led to the outbreak of universal disruption and discord.

During the painful process of discord, however the ability to maintain a cosmic bond to the outer space connection was not completely lost. Although the mainstream of our society experienced a decline in the level of spirituality, a small minority of spiritual people have always appeared on the scene and carried on the knowledge of universal intelligence. The scientific transformation we now experience, both in depth and magnitude suggests a need for a deep reexamination of our basic world view of the universe, and hopefully a reconceptualizing of basic concepts leading to a holistic framework of our physical reality.

Let us now return to the Zohar for an incredible account of possible future warfare, that, from the Kabbalistic world view of our universe, may and hopefully will be prevented from taking place.

"Now where was Balaam at that time? Seeing that he said, 'Now I am going to my people'[232] how can he have been in Midian? The truth is that when he saw that twenty-four thousand Israelites perished, by his counsel, he stayed there and demanded his reward: and while he was staying there Pinhas and his captains of the hosts came there. When Balaam saw Pinhas he flew up into the air with his two sons Yunus and Yumburus. But these two, you will say, died at the time when the Golden Calf was made. In fact with their supernatural powers they produced a *living* golden calf.[233] Balaam, however, being acquainted with every kind of witchcraft, took also the knowledge of his sons, and began to fly away.

When Pinhas saw a man in the air flying away, he shouted to his soldiers: Is anyone able to fly after him, for it is Balaam? Then Zilya, of the tribe of Dan, arose and seized the root, source of energy of the dominion of witchcraft, the power which rules over all extensions of sorcery and witchcraft and flew after him. When Balaam saw him he changed his direction in the air, (warp-nine) and broke through five levels of galaxies and vanished from view, Zilya was then sorely vexed, not knowing what to do. Pinhas called out after tapping the cosmic connection of the Tree of Life and ordered the Ruler of the dragons which overshadow all serpents to sever all infusion of cosmic power to Balaam. The metaphysical command by Pinhas brought Balaam in view, whereupon Zilya approached him and brought him down in front of Pinhas.

When Balaam came down in front of Pinhas, he said to him: Wretch, how many evil haps hast thou brought upon the holy people! Pinhas then said to Zilya: Kill him, but *not* with the cosmic Name, for it is not fitting that Balaam meet his fate by the divine sanctity of the Holy Name, The reason for this is to prevent his (Balaam), soul when

leaving him, from becoming united with higher levels of spiritual, holy cosmic energy forces, and his (Balaam) prayer fulfilled: "May
my soul die the death of the righteous."[234] He then tried to kill him in
many ways, but did not succeed, until he took a sword on which was
engraved a snake on each side. Said Pinhas: Kill him with his own
weapon. And then he did kill him; for such is the way of that side, he
who follows it is killed by it and it is with his soul when it departs from
him. One who lives by and connects with cosmic negative energy
forces ultimately meets death at the hand of this very same energy
force, in as much as cosmic negative energy is an intelligent energy
force, similarly as the all inclusive positive cosmic force. As an intelligent energy force, negative cosmic forces have no purpose or
direction but to heap distruction on whatever comes in contact with
it."[235] It is the kind of robot that does not learn to be selective in its objective, and if turned towards its master can successfully annihilate
the very essence and cause of its own existence. If an employer
teaches his employer how to steal from his competition, that very
same employee one day will turn around and steal from his teacher.
The innate characteristic of positive energy is to extend out and
duplicate the cause of its essence which is one of sharing, whereas,
negative energy tends to turn inwards, the aspect of the desire to
receive without regard to other entities.

The difficulty in maintaining the concept of "love thy neighbor as
thy self"[236] in our society lies precisely in our inability to accept the
presence of others. First and foremost, is the self guided by a cosmic
energy intelligence of negativity, a universal problem. The price that
humankind pays for its link to cosmic negativity is far to high and we
can ill afford to continue or remain on our present stage of human suffering. The principle of cause and effect dictates the life process of our
universe. Consequently, Pinhas recognized the necessity of using the
very same cosmic weapon in ridding the world of so powerful a
negative individual as Balaam.

The past ten years have taught us to be cautious with the word "impossible." Human travel beyond our own solar universe is a stagger-
ing realization, a concept that most of us do not really expect to come
about in our lifetime. The fundamental problem lies in inadequate

propulsion which seems to have limited humankind to our planet. Alternative methods are necessary to reduce time travel to figures compatible with our life span. Consequently, travel speeds necessary to meet this requirement would have to approach or exceed the speed of light.

The Zohar apparently does not consider the problems connected with approaching the speed of light as the singular obstacle in achieving human travel beyond our solar system, inasmuch as the problem does not lie in producing such speeds that would take infinite propulsion power to accelerate an object beyond the light barrier. The crisis facing the scientist today is Einstein's theory of relativity, which has withstood the test of critical experiment and which indicates that the inertia of propulsion of mass of an object can approach infinity only when the object approaches the speed of light, and it is impossible to exceed the speed of light.

Amazingly enough, the Zohar presents a plan that will provide man with the capability of turning the entire solar system, including terrestrial Earth, into a human backyard, no less than the airplane effect which converted the once formidable oceans into little more than swimming holes.

The solution lies, not in effectively producing propulsion that will approach the speed of light beyond the light barrier, but rather in simply *removing the barrier itself*. This concept has been hinted at within the many recorded accounts mentioned in both the Bible and the Zohar. Eerie as this may sound, it is all in perfect harmony with the new age ideas concerning the laws of space and time.[237] There is no fundamental reason why the world of physics cannot creat a new renaissance that will open up the *whole* solar system to humankind transportation, as so stated in the Zohar.[238] No new revolutionary discoveries are really required because, basically, Einstein's apparent proof that we cannot drive starships faster than the speed of light is not and should not be considered as the only real obstacle in the future.

The answer is, as so clearly and simply stated in the Zohar, that the removal of the *light barrier* completely depends upon the removal of the humankind barrier, represented by hate and intolerance for each other. This feat, of overcoming the obstacles of space travel and the light barrier was clearly demonstrated by both the prophet Elijah and Pinhas, who were actually one and the same person.[239]

Both knew and understood where to look in the hazy forest of light barriers and thereby knew how to dissect the anatomy of interstellar flight.

In summary, with present scientific knowledge, we should be able to respond to the challenge of stellar space exploration. Recognizing the formidable obstacle which stands in our way, which is the concept of "Love thy neighbor as thy would thyself."

The kabbalistic world view of essential reality reflects the innate harmonious interrelatedness of our universe. To achieve a state of dynamic balance, a cultural revolution, in a sense will be needed. The dissipation of the light barrier in particular, and I might add, the survival or our entire galaxy may very well depend on whether we can bring about a unified whole of mankind. The removal of physical barriers depends completely on our ability to remove our metaphysical barriers of intolerance and hatred. The universe no longer can be viewed as a machine consisting of a multitude of physical objects alone, but more importantly, must be seen as one dynamic whole where non-physical entities such as the thought processes, the nature of consciousness are essentially part of and related to the universal whole.

Furthermore, metaphysical manifestations are always regarded as the primary reality and essence which manifest themselves ultimately as a web of material, physical patterns. To be more precise, it is the manifestation of thought that precedes the emergence of material patterns. The world must be viewed as a complicated web of infinite events, material and non-material, that determine the tissue of the whole.

Then and only then, can we understand the dynamic interplay of our cosmos, where in the kabbalistec world view of cosmic reality, the conceptual tissue of tolerance may be the all important factor in determining the substance of the whole . Cosmic consciousness, astral influences are very much a part of the universal thread of our cosmic order.

12

The Revolution of Change

The only constant phenomena of civilization is change.
— Philip S. Berg

T RADITION IS A RESPECTABLE WORD, BUT IT NO LONGER HAS ANY place in the lexicon of science, finance, or government. Just as we are in the throes of a world-wide revolution in communication systems, international cooperation, social reforms, examples of how seriously repressive long established patterns of thought can be are all to familiar. Technology, especially electronics, is becoming obsolete at an ever increasing rate. The science of physics has emerged as an uncertainly principle. Change is inevitable.

The only constant known to mankind is change.

Interestingly enough, the revolving wheel of change never seems to come to an end, and the economic, and social burdens that result from the ending of an old cycle of life must be balanced with the enormous weight of the unknown that comes with a new cycle. We seem to be at a critical crossroad where meaning and significance have little to offer by way of gaining an understanding of how to be one with the universe. The risk of change, whether social or economic, in the past 20 years has proved to be extremely hazardous, and does not seem to have rescued the problems brought by change in terms of family, traditions and cultural breakdown. There is a striking parallel between the dramatic changes brought by the microchip to the electronic and computer industries and the disastrous transformation social disorder will bring to a world plagued by problems of drugs and environmental pollution. Both have dramatically increased man's alienation from himself and his culture. The former has almost reduced the initiative of man to a robotic consciousness, whereas the latter has thrust man into a feeling of isolation and an inability to communicate with his fellows. Reduction of matter in technology has brought a greater awareness of the internal, sub-atomic level of interrelatedness whereas social and moral disintegration has strengthened the hand of isolation, where time-proven values and moral standards which have been supportive of relationships, are crumbling and becoming meaningless to our society as a whole. The interrelatedness of humankind appears to be running a course quite contrary to the internal field of inanimate matter, which with increasing technological progress, continues to point to an interrelatedness of the all-embracing unity.

Many sociologists and government planners have expressed deep concern about our ability to respond properly should continuous disintegration of our social structure trigger the need for dramatic increase in social welfare. Some of the issues being the high rate of unemployment and, a higher incidence of the divorce rate. This is the key issue among many relating to the deeper needs of man, no matter how much comfort the material sciences may give to the physical body.

Does change hold lessons for mankind? What is lacking is a proper sense of perspective; of the real contribution which modern technology as a whole has made to human well being. At the same time, there is a failure to understand that change cannot always perform miracles and that the inevitable risks which must accompany change must also be accepted. It is perhaps too much to ask of ourselves, that we should, strike this balance inasmuch as we have conditioned ourselves to demand the best for our material needs, without necessarily considering the responsibilities of such change.

All of this poses a serious problem for science of Astrology. Traditionally, the search for the cosmic connection, left to astrologers, has been dismissed as superstition by the scientific community. One of the problems relates to the recent discovery of three new planets, — Uranus in 1781, Neptune in 1846 and Pluto in 1930. Because of these discoveries conventional astrology recently has undergone changes. Aries and Scorpio, once were ruled by Mars, but Scorpio now is considered a cosmic entity under Pluto, and Pisces now finds conventional astrology attributing the planet Neptune as ruler over Pisces. Saturn, that "old father time" planet once considered the cosmic ruler of Capricorn and Aquarius, suddenly is subject to change and we find the sign Aquarius ruled by Uranus.

From a Kabbalistic world view of our universe, these three newly discovered planets will not in any way change the course of astral influences that have been established from its very inception. It is only when we treat a planet from its outward, external cosmic energy aspect that we tend to believe that with its discovery greater awareness and greater recognition of the astral influences of planets by man take place.

R. Shimon said, "I raised my head in prayer to the supernal Whole, that the wisdom of the Kabbalah be revealed by me within the terrestrial lower world, as it was concealed within my heart. We do not make use of the external knowledge, but rather the in-depth sublime path of the coded Bible is our source reference. The seven planetary bodies, that are in constant motion, which are referred to by names of a lower, external dimension, namely, Saturn, Jupiter, Mars, Sun, Venus, Mercury, and the Moon are symbolic and directed by its seven internal cosmic influences, which are concealed from the knowledge of conventional astrology. These seven astral forces are the seven sefirot of Mercy, Judgement, Beauty, Victory, Splendor, Foundation and Kingdom. The internal energy force does not undergo any changes. The external body energy force is subjected to change and consequently creates confusion in its physical expression."[240]

The language, the knowledge of astrology will not undergo any change along with the usual progressive change in human and technical development. What merely emerges from the human development as well as the technical development is merely to permit us to grow with greater consciousness, become more aware of the validity of the existence of the laws and principles established by either conventional astrology or Kabbalistic astrology. But Kabbalistic astrology is not subject to new discovery because the root of its development has already been known since the time of Abraham. Consequently, the new revelations and new manifestations will no way affect the astral influence that will take place in our universe. If changes are taking place, they are taking place because the celestial bodies are taking on new positions; those positions are merely for the observance of what changes might be taking place on a manifested, external physical level.

Our concern and the objective of this book is to become conscious with a pure awareness of total knowledge by which we can then affect, not changes in celestial bodies, but rather to make certain that negative cosmic energies will not excercise the kind of influence that it has in the past.

With the dawning of the Age of Aquarius and as man moves closer to a more universal humanitarian relationship, so will the sciences begin to recognize the more subtle, internal interrelationships between man and the cosmos. As the internal relationships between man evolve and become more fully developed, so will more of the invisible world become visible to the science and the ultimate interrelationship seen at its sub-cosmic level. . . .

References

Introduction
1. Psalms, ch. 19:2-3.
2. Einstein, Essays in Science.
3. Kabbalah for the Layman, Berg, pp. 76-82.
4. Ten Luminous Emanations, Vol. 2, R. Yehuda Ashlag, Research Centre of Kabbalah, p. 19-21.
5. John Wheeler, The Physicists Conception of Nature.
6. Zohar II, p. 171a.
7. Zohar I, p 134b.
8. Ibid., p. 134b.
9. Ibid., p. 134b.
10. Genesis, ch. 1:16-19.
11. Ibid., ch. 29:32-35, ch. 30.
12. Numbers, ch. 2:2,3.
13. Genesis, ch.1:14.

Chapter 1
14. Genesis, ch. 4:1.
15. The Kabbalah Connection, Berg, p. 30.
16. Gates of Reincarnation, R. Isaac Luria, p. 136.
17. Entrance to the Zohar, R. Yehuda Ashlag, ed. Berg, pp. 110-116. Entrance to the Tree of Life, R. Yehuda Ashlag, ed. Berg, pp. 127-131.
18. Two Kinds of Reality, pp. 197-198.
19. Werner Heisenberg, Physics and Philosophy, p. 200.
20. Kabbalah for the Layman, Berg, pp. 101-104

Chapter 2
21. Ezekiel, ch. 38:1-23.
22. Genesis, ch 5,6.
23. Numbers, ch. 13:33, Genesis, ch. 6:4.
24. Zohar I, p. 71a. Ibid: p. 53a-b.
25. Zohar I, p. 134b.
26. Gates of Reincarnation, R. Isaac Luria, p. 136. Kabbalah for the Layman, Berg, pp. 38-41. Zohar II, p. 141b.

27. Zohar I, p. 134b.
28. Zohar II, p. 265a.
29. Zohar III, p. 281b.
30. Zohar II, p. 171a. Ibid. p. 203a.
31. Ibid., p. 203a.
32. Exodus, ch. 35:1-3.
33. Zohar II, p. 7a-8a.
34. Sefer Yetzirah,
35. Zohar II, p. 8a-10a.
36. Leviticus, h. 19:18.
37. Zohar I, p. 134b.
38. Zohar II, p. 10a.

Chapter 3
39. Numbers, ch. 2:1,2.
40. Zohar III, 281b.
41. Isaiah, ch. 29:14.
42. Zohar I, p. 195b.
43. Ecclesiastes, ch. 1:8, ch. 7.
44. Zohar I, p. 195b.
45. Zohar II, p. 191a.
46. Exodus.
47. Zohar II, p. 191a.
48. Werner Heisenberg, Physics and Philosophy, p. 58.
49. Neils Bohr, Atomic Physics and the Description of Nature, p. 2.
50. Zohar I, p. 180b.
51. Zohar III, p. 281b.
52. Ibid. III, p. 101b.
53. Song of Songs, ch. 1:7.
54. Ibid, ch. 1:7.
55. Genesis, ch. 1:14.
56. Amos, ch. 7:2.
57. Samuel I, ch. 15:17.
58. Genesis, ch. 12:1.
59. Zohar III, p. 281b.
60. Talmud Bavli, Tractate Hulin, p. 60b.
61. Genesis, ch. 1:16.
62. Zohar III, p. 181a.
63. Isaiah, ch. 57:15.
64. Psalms, ch. 34:19.
65. Zohar I, p. 195a.
66. Ecclesiastes, ch. 1:8-11.
67. Ibid., ch. 3:11.
68. Ibid., ch. 3:12.

69. Zohar I, p. 195b.
70. Ecclesiastes, ch. 9:12.
71. Ibid., ch. 3:1-8.

Chapter 4
72. Micah, ch. 5:6.
73. Zohar I, p. 203b.
74. Numbers, ch. 24:17.
75. Zohar II, p. 7a-10a.
76. Numbers, ch. 24:14.
77. Talmud Bavli, Tractate Berakhat, p. 58b.

Chapter 5
78. Light Waves and Their Uses, Albert A. Michelson, pp. 23-24.
79. Walter Meissner, Max Planck, The Man and His World.
80. Kabbalah for the Layman, Berg, p. 70-83.
81. Shabbat Hymn, Leha Dodi, R. Shlomo Alkabetz.
82. Talmud Bavli, Tractate Nedarim, p. 32a.
83. Talmud Bavli, Tractate Pesahim, p. 113b.
84. Talmud Bavli, Tractate Shabbat, p. 156a.
85. Jeremiah, ch. 10:2.
86. Talmud Bavli, Tractate Moed Katan,
87. Genesis, ch. 15:5.
88. Zohar I, p. 90a-b.
89. Zohar II, p. 171a.
90. Zohar I, p. 53a.
91. Zohar II, p. 171b.
92. An Entrance to the Zohar, R. Yehuda Ashlag, ed. Berg, pp. 110116.
93. Tree of Life, R. Isaac Luria, Research Centre of Kabbalah, edition 1985, Gate 42, Sec. 1.
94. Deuteronomy, ch. 32:49.
95. Ibid., ch. 34:1.
96. Zohar III, p. 157a.
97. Psalms, ch. 19:2.
98. Genesis, ch. 1:17.

Chapter 6
99. Genesis, ch. 2:19.
100. Ibid., ch. 12:1-3.
101. Ibid., ch. 15:2-4.
102. Kabbalah for the Layman, Berg, pp. 71-74.
101. Genesis, ch. 15:6.
102. Ibid., ch. 17:5,15.
103. Ibid., ch. 12:1-3.
104. Kabbalah for the Layman, Berg, p. 55.
105. Job, ch. 4:8.
106. Zohar III, p. 110b.
107. Psalms, ch. 37:3.
108. Proverbs, ch. 10:2.
109. Leviticus, ch. 19:18.
110. Wheels of a Soul, Berg, pp. 58-59.
111. Jeremiah, ch. 1:4-5.
112. Zohar I, p.201a.
113. Proverbs, ch. 20:5.
114. Kabbalah Connection, Berg, pp. 117, 118.
115. Zohar I, p. 201b.
116. Zohar III, p. 15a.
117. Amos, ch. 3:7.
118. Psalms, ch. 11:8.

Chapter 7
119. Zohar I, p. 133b.
120. Genesis, ch. 25:1.
121. Kings, ch. 1:5-10.
122. Kabbalah for the Layman, Berg, pp. 100-102.
123. Jeremiah, ch. 31:33.
124. Genesis, ch. 4:1. Kabbalah Connection, Berg, pp. 154-157.

Chapter 8
125. Deuteronomy, ch. 16:1.
126. Kabbalah Connection, Berg, pp. 142-146.
127. Kabbalah Connection, Berg, pp. 130-132.
128. Exodus, ch. 7:19.
129. Ibid., ch. 12:2.
130. Kabbalah Connection, Berg, p. 107.

131. Kabbalah for the Layman, Berg, pp. 71-74.
132. Zohar I, p. 15a.
133. Kabbalah for the Layman, pp. 101-104.
134. Exodus, ch. 12:7.
135. Zohar II, p. 39b.
136. Kabbalah Connection, Berg, pp. 148-152.
137. Zohar II, p. 39b.
138. Exodus, ch. 12:6.
139. Leviticus, ch. 25:55.
140. Kabbalah for the Layman, Berg, p. 55-58.
141. Zohar II, p. 32b.
142. Zohar III, p. 282a, Zohar I, p. 119a.
143. Kabbalah for the Layman, Berg, pp. 81-82.
144. Zohar I, p. 119a.
145. Zachariah, ch. 14:2.
146. Zohar I, p. 119a.
147. Ibid., p. 119a.
148. Isaiah, ch. 66:20.
149. Zohar I, p. 119a.
150. Zohar II, p. 17b.
151. Joshua, ch. 10:11.
152. Exodus, ch. 9:18.
153. Ibid., ch. 9:24.
154. Talmud Bavli, Tractate Berahhat, p. 54b.
155. Numbers, ch. 16:32.
156. Isaiah, ch. 13:10-13.
157. Ibid., ch. 24:18-20.
158. Zohar I, p. 107b.

Chapter 9
159. Joshua, ch. 10:14.
160. Zohar II, p. 198b.
161. Exodus, ch. 14:27.
162. Zohar II, p. 49a.
163. Rashi, Exodus, ch. 14:21.
164. Exodus, ch. 12:1-2.
165. Nahmanides, Perush Ha'Ramban, Exodus, ch. 12:2.
166. Exodus, ch. 20:2.
167. Ibid., ch. 20:13.

168. Ibid., ch. 12:29.
169. Kabbalah Connection, Berg, pp. 110-116.
170. Ibid., p. 185.
171. Kitvay Ari, Lekutai Torah, p. 138.
172. Exodus, ch. 13:3,4.
173. Rashi, Exodus, ch. 13:3.
174. Kabbalah Connection, Berg, pp. 164-167.
175. Genesis, ch. 4:1.

Chapter 10
176. Exodus, ch. 13:21.
177. Zohar II, p. 46a.
178. Zohar I, p. 75b.
179. Daniel, ch. 2:20.
180. Ezekiel, ch. 36:27.
181. Ibid., ch. 20:18.
182. Ibid., ch. 1:14.
183. Talmud Bavli, Tractate Hagigah, p. 13a.
184. Kabbalah for the Layman, Berg, pp. 94-101.
185. Genesis Rabbah, ch. 82:6.
186. Ezekiel, ch. 1:16.
187. Ibid., ch. 1:16-20.
188. Zohar Hadash, p. 39, Section 3-4.
189. Judges, ch. 5:4-5.
190. Psalms, 68:9.
191. Ezekiel, ch. 1:15.
192. Zohar I, p. 124b.
193. Ibid., p. 124b.
194. Ibid., p. 55a.

Chapter 11
195. Kabbalah Connection, Berg, p. 117.
196. Genesis, ch. 2:7.
197. Zohar I, p. 49a.
198. Kabbalah Connection, Berg, p. 117, 118.
199. Genesis, ch. 5:1.
200. Zohar I, p. 376a.
201. Zohar III, p. 124b.
202. Deuteronomy, ch. 31:16.
203. Isaiah, ch. 11:9.

204. Jeremiah, ch. 31:34.
205. Zohar III, p. 95a.
206. Deuteronomy, ch. 34:7.
207. Zohar I, p. 37b.
208. Isaiah, ch. 65:22.
209. Deuteronomy, ch. 34:6.
210. II Kings, ch. 2:8-12.
211. Tikune Zohar, p. 1a.
212. Zohar I, p. 38a.
213. Joshua, ch. 5:13-15,ch. 6:2-6.
214. Exodus, ch. 25:16.
215. II Samuel, ch. 6:6,7.
216. Exodus, ch. 14:21.
217. Mehilta, ch. 14:21.
218. Tree of Life, R. Isaac Luria, Yeshuvat Kol Yehuda, ch. 42, Section 8.
219. Targum Yerushalmi, Exodus, ch. 14:22.
220. Numbers, ch. 22:2.
221. Zohar III, p. 184b.
222. Numbers, ch. 21:28.

223. Zohar III, p. 184b.
224. Jeremiah, ch. 31:33.
225. Kabbalah Connection, Berg, p. 165.
226. Kabbalah for the Layman, Berg, p. 128.
227. Zohar III, p. 193b.
228. Numbers ch. 31:8.
229. Exodus, ch. 29:36.
230. Deuteronomy, ch. 34:10.
231. Proverbs, ch. 27:2.
232. Numbers, ch. 24:14.
233. Exodus, ch. 32:1-6.
234. Numbers, ch. 23:10.
235. Zohar III, p. 194a-b.
236. Leviticus, ch. 19:14.
237. Kabbalah Connection, Berg, p. 34.
238. Zohar III, p. 194b.
239. Ibid., p. 282a.

Chapter 12
240. Zohar III, p. 287a.

Biographical
Notes

Abarbanel, R. Don Isaac (b. Lisbon 1437, d. Venice 1509). Rediscovered the wondrous world of the mystical realm in general and the Kabbalah in particular. Served the Spanish royal house before the expulsion of the Jews from Spain. He succeeded in piercing the iron curtain concealing the mysterious enigmas of redemption cloaked in the Book of Daniel. He offered encouragement to Jews following their expulsion from Spain by composing several works concerned with the central desire of the period, the coming of the Messiah.

Abraham Ben David of Posqueres, known as the Rabad (c. 1125-1198). A master scholar in Montpelliar and Vimes. A keen and resourceful and undisputed master in his own field. Highly knowledgeable in related areas, as philosophy and philology. Many of his theories and insights were transmitted by subsequent generations of talmudists and incorporated in standard works of Jewish, up to the Shulhan Arukh and its later commentaries.

Aboab, Isaac (end of the 14th century). Spanish rabbinic author and preacher. His work, Menorat Hamoar is one of the most popular works of religious edification amongst the Jews in the middle ages. In his book Menorat Hamoar, he discusses the underlying reasons of general practices combining the teachings of Maimonides with the ideas of Kabbalah.

Abraham Bar Hiyyah (d.c. 1136 Spain). Together with Abraham Ibn Ezra took a positive position towards astrology and even based his practical affairs on astrological considerations. He also brought proof from the Talmud that the Rabbis of that time agreed in principle with the non-Jewish sages differing only in that saying "that the stars impel but do not compel."

Abraham Ibn Ezra (1089-1164, Toledo, Spain). His reputation spread beyond the Jewish world. He believed that although everything in this universe is under the influence of the planets and signs of the Zodiac, it is within the power of man to free himself of their dictates by perfecting himself. Ibn Ezra composed many works on astrology. His writings have been translated into Latin at the close of the 13th century and printed in 1507. Some of his works are: Reshit Hokhmah, Mishpitai Ha'Mazalot, Sefer Ha'Teamim and Sefer Ha'Meorot.

Abraham, Patriarch-Genesis, (1900 B.C.E.). First known astrologer to be aware that man has the ability to transcend cosmic influences. The Sefer Yetzirah, the first known work on astrology, was authored by him. A most important kabbalistic astrology work referred to frequently in the Zohar and other kabbalistic works.

Adam. Considered to have been created with absolute awareness and knowledge of all the secrets of the universe. Books attributed to Adam are Sefer Toldoth Ha'Adam and Sefer Raziel Hamalakh, many sections dealing with astrology.

Aderet, Salomon ben Abraham (c.b. 1235 Barcelona; d. 1310). Also known as the RASHBA, acronym for his full name, famous for his talmudical commentaries, poetry, philosophy and lesser known for his Kabbalistic writings. Student of R. Jonah Gerondi and Nahmanides.

Alcorsono Judah ben Joseph (14th century). Morocean theological scholar. For unknown reasons he was put in prison where he wrote Aron Ha-Edut (Ark of Testimony) on such subjects as Ma'aseh Bereshit and Ma'aseh Uerkovah. The story of the Garden of Eden, providence, prophecy and Satan's dispute with God. The work is divided into 22 chapters corresponding to the number of letters in the Hebrew alphabet. In Saadiah ben Maemon ibn Danan's Maamar al seder ha Dorot, Alcorsono is mentioned as an astrologer.

Aldabi Meir ben Isaac (Toledo c.1310-c.1360). Religious philosopher with strong leanings toward the Kabbalah. Later settled in Jerusalem where in 1360 he finished his long contemplated astronomical work: Shevilei Emunah (Path of Faith) first published in Riva di Trento, 1518.

Alhadib Isaac ben Solomon (Spain 1396-1429). Hebrew poet and astronomer. His writings in astronomy are Iggeret Kelei Hemdah, describing an astronomical apparatus which he invented in Sicily, Keli Haemzai.

Alshekh Moses ben Hayim (d. after 1593). Salonica; later Safed. Prominent Kabbalistic authority, talmudic teacher and preacher. Ordained in 1590 by Hayim Vital. Wrote commetaries on most of the books of the Bible, as: Harazzdet Ha Sharon (Constantinople 1563: Venice

1591), Shoghanat Ha Amakim (Venice 1591), Rav Peninim (Venice 1592) and more.

He also wrote commentaries on the astrological book Yesod Olam by Isaac ben Joseph Israeli.

Attar, R. Hayyim (b. 1696 Morocco d. 1743 Jerusalem). Kabbalist who became famous for his best known and important commentary on the bible, Or Ha-Hayyim (Light of Life), based entirely on Kabbalistic teachings. In 1741, settled in Jerusalem and established an academy of learning. His yarzeit is celebrated by many thousands of Jews each year in Jerusalem.

Azulai, R. Abraham ben Mordchai (1570-1643). Famous Kabbalist born in Fez from a family of Kabbalists of Castilian origin, wrote three treatises on the Zohar; Or Levanah (Light of the Moon), Or ha-Chamah (Light of the Sun), and Or-ha-Ganuz (the Hidden Light), based primarily on the Lurianic system. Underscored the permission granted for *all* to enter the gates of the world of mysticism.

Bahir (Sefer ha-Bahir). The book Bahir together with the Zohar was widely known in the thirteenth century in Spain. Authorship attributed to R. Nehunia ben ha-Kana. As the Zohar means "splendor," so this work Bahir means "brightness." Contains interpretations of letters and sounds, parables and mystical ideas linked to the Torah, following the profound explanations of the Zohar.

Bahya ben Asher ben Hlava (13th century). Spanish Kabbalist famous for his commentary on the Bible and numerous works on the Kabbalah, disciple of Solomon b. Abraham Aderet. Preacher and Kabbalist, some of his books are: Ha Emuza ve Ha Bittachon (Koretz 1785), Maarechet Ha Elohut (Mantua 1558) and Maamar Ha Shekhel (Gerona 1557).

Bahya, R. Ibn Pakuda (c. 1080–1170). Kabbalist and philosopher who lived in Spain, author of the famous work Havot ha-levavot (Duties of the Heart).

Bar Yohai Rabi Shimeon (Zohar). Some 1300 years before Copernicus the

Zohar states "The whole Earth spins in a circle, like a ball, the one part is up, while the other part is down. The one part is light while the other is dark . . . ."

Ben Zakai Rabi Johanan (c. 50 A.D.). Youngest disciple of Hillel who foresaw the destruction of the Temple (Tractate Yuma 39b), concluded that the establishment of a Torah centre was the last and only hope for the Jews to exist as a nation without the binding force of the Holy Temple. He was smuggled out of Jerusalem as a corpse by his students R. Eliezer ben Hyrcanus and R. Joshua ben Hananiah, and presented himself before the Roman commander Vespasian asking his permission to establish a Torah academy in Yavneh. (Tractate Gitin 55b.) His request granted, Yavneh became the spiritual centre of Jewish life where the Great Sanhedrin was reestablished. The subjects taught by him were Halachah and Aggadah — ethics and reasons for the commandments Maaseh Bereshit and Maaseh Merkava.

Barzillai, Judah ben Al-Bargeloni (12th century). Spanish Kabbalist and halachist known for his commentary on the Sefer Yetzirah called Perush Sefer Yetzirah. His other works include Sefer ha-Ittim, which deals with the Jewish festivals which are referred to extensively by later commentaries.

Botarel, Moses ben Isaac (15th century). Spanish Kabbalist, whose main work is a commentary on the Sefer Yetzirah. This invaluable work stemmed from his desire to enhance the status of Kabbalism.

Cordovero, R. Moses (1522–1570). Also known by the abbreviation REMAK, famed Kabbalist of Safeds' "golden age", brother-in-law of R. Shlomo Alkabetz, and one-time teacher of the Ari, R. Luria. His large main work "Ohr Yakar", (Precious Light), on the entire Zohar has only recently begun to see the light of day. Originator of one of the two basic systems of understanding the Zohar. His other major work 'Pardes Remmonim' (Garden of Pomegranates) is a systematic compendium of Kabbalistic concepts surrounding the internal action of the original unified energy force emanating from the Creator. R. Haim Vital, student of R. Yitzchak Luria, had a dream in which the Remak revealed to him, that in the age of the Messiah the Lurianic system would prevail.

Crescas, Hasdai (b. 1340 Barcelona; d. 1412 Zaragoza). Famed Spanish Kabbalist and philosopher whose criticism of Jewish Aristotelianism provided a stimulus for and paved the way to an in depth recognition of the internal, metaphysical world of reality. His main work was "Or-Adonai (The Light of G-d) in which he presented his criticism of Jewish Aristotelianism. Together with Joseph Albo, was of the opinion that: in view of human free will and divine providence, it is impossible to contribute an absolute decisive character to "the dictates of the configuration."

Donolo Shabbatai (c. 913–982). Famed Italian Kabbalist and physician who was born in Oria, Italy. His most famous work on Kabbalah is his book "Sefer Hakhmoni", a commentary on the Sefer yetzirah. His Sefer Ha-Mirkahot (Book of Remedies) drew material from his knowledge of "Hakarot Hapartzuf" (physiognomies) and astrology, which undoubtedly was based on his comprehension of the Kabbalah. His Sefer Hakhmoni provides a massive collection of information regarding the study of astronomy; without it , the study of astrology would remain imcomprehensible.

Ezra ben Solomon (d. 1238 or 1245). One of the leading Kabbalists of his day in Gerona, Spain. For a long time scholars thought him identical with Azriel b. Menahem of Gerona. According to Abrahamm Abulafia, Ezra wrote a commentary to the Sefer Yezirah.

Falaquera, Nathan ben Joel (late 13th century). Spanish physician. He may be identical with Nathan of Montpellier, the teacher of the author of Sefer Hayashar, Rabbeinu Tam (the Tossafot). He considered astrology a true science and made use of it.

Galante, R. Abraham (c. 1570). Famed Safed Kabbalist of the sixteenth century, known for his commentary on the Zohar.

Galico, R. Elisha. Famed Kabbalist of the sixteenth century, known for his commentary on the Zohar. Member of the Rabbinical Court of R. Yosef Karo in Safed.

Gaon of Vilna (1720–1797). ha-Gaon R. Eliyahu (abreviated ha-Gra), famous for his Kabbalistic writings which number some eighty volumes, halachist of the Talmud.

Gerondi, R. Moses ben Solomon D'escola (b. 1244, Gerona; d. 1263, Toledo). Cousin of Nahmanides, famous for ethical writings, "Shaarei Teshuvah" and "Sefer ha-Yira".

Gershom ben Solomon (13th century). Provençal scholar of Beziers. Wrote halachic works, as well as a book called Shaar Ha Shamaim that contains sections of the works of Ptolemy, Aristotle, Avicenna and Averroes. Highly estimated in the Middle ages. Meir Aldabi (c. 1360) used it extensively in the astronomical section of his book Shevilei Emunah.

Gikatila, R. Joseph (c. 1270). Famed Spanish Kabbalist whose writings Ginnath Egoz (Garden of Nut Trees), Iggereth ha-Kodesh (Holy Letter) and Shaare Orah (Gates of Light) provided a systematic development to the internal structure and meaning of symbolism.

Halevi, Judah (1075–1141, Toleda, Spain). Never took a definite stand concerning the value of reliability of astrology. He admitted (Kuzari 4:9) that the celestial bodies had an influence over terrestrial affairs, that terrestrial life was due to changing constellations, and that all astrological sayings attributed to the rabbis of old were based on genuine traditions.

Hayim, R. Kohen (c. 1600). Famed Kabbalist of Aleppo, student of R. Hayim Vital, composer of mystical hymns in the form of dialogues between the Creator and Israel.

Hayim Vital, R. (b. 1543 Safed; d. Damascus 1620). The selected student of R. Isaac Luria, the Ari, who together with his son Shmuel accepted the task of recording the Ari's thoughts on paper.

Isaac ben Joseph Israeli (Toledo, first half of the 14th century). Spanish astronomer best known for his book Yesod Oham (written in 1310) a study of astronomy and cosmography highly estimated over several centuries. Commentaries on his work were written by Alhadib — Judah Bassan and Elijah Mizrachi. He is also the author of two other books: Shaar Hashamaim and Shaar Hamilu'im.

Ibn Gaon, Shem Tov ben Abraham (late 13th to 14th centuries). Spanish Kabbalist and halakhist whose teacher was Solomon ben Abraham

Aderet. His best known work on the Kabbalah is "Keter Shem Tov" and "Migdal Oz", a commentary on the Mishneh Torah of Maimonides.

Ibn Habib, Jacob ben Solomon (c. 1440–1515). Rabbinical scholar born in Castile, Spain; heading a yeshivah which was one of the largest in Spain. On the expulsion of the Jews from Spain he went to Portugal and then on to Salonika, which had become the main centre for the study of Kabbalah. His most famous work, Ein Yakov, in which he assembled the aggadot of the Babylonian and Jerusalem Talmud.

Ibn Motot, Samuel ben Saadiah (c. 1370). Spanish Kabbalist and was one of the inner circle of Spanish Kabbalists in Castile.

Ibn Shem Tov, Shem Tov (c. 1380–1440). Spanish Kabbalist, known as the anti-Maimonidean Kabbalist.

Ibn Waqar, Joseph ben Abraham (c. 14th century). Kabbalist who lived in Toledo, Spain and formulated his Kabbalistic ideas through his now famous poem, Shir ha-Yihud.

Isaac ben Todros of Barcelona (14th century). Spanish Kabbalist and student of Nahmanides whose teachings are included among the writings of the disciples of Nahmanides.

Isaac the Blind (c. 1200). Famous Spanish Kabbalist who lived in Provence, son of the famed Kabbalist, Rabbi Abraham ben David of Posquieres.

Ishmael, R. ben Elisha. Famous Tanna of the first and second centuries, c.e., contemporary of Rabbi Akiba and among the martyrs of the Hadrian persecution in 135 c.e. He won for himself a permanent place as a figure in Jewish mysticism with his explanations of the twenty two letters of the Hebrew alphabet as discribed in his "Baraita de R. Ishmael". He also authored Thirteen Principles of Logic.

Joseph Ibn-Tabul. Kabbalist living in Safed (c. 16th century) who taught the Lurianic system of Kabbalah.

Judah ben Solomon Ha Kohen Ibn Matkah of Toledo (first half 13th century, Toledo). Spanish philosphical writer. Disciple of Abulafia in 1245. He wrote in Arabic an encyclopedic work on logic, physics, metaphysics, geometry and astronomy based on writings of Aristotle, Euclid and Ptolemy. Called Midrash Ha Hokhmah — part of which consists of summaries of the great Greek and Muslim astronomers.

Karo, R. Joseph (b. 1488, Spain; d. 1575, Safed). Author of the "Shulkhan Arukh" the most authoritative codification of Jewish law, and great Rabbinical authority of the sixteenth century. Also known for his Kabbalistic writing "Magid Meshurim" which contains visions and revelations only attributable to a Kabbalist.

Levi ben Gershon (1288–1344). Acronym RalBaG. Maintained that the activities and events of a man's life were predestined by the positions and movements of celestial bodies. The astrologers fail, he asserted, first because of insufficient knowledge about the movements of the stars and their influence, and because of the intervention of intellect and free will. Astrology book Milhamot Adonae an astronomical treatise of 136 chapters.

Leon R. Moses de ben Shemtov (c. 1290). Famed Kabbalist in Spain who revealed for the first time the existence of a physical instrument that can provide spiritual insights to the five books of Moses, the Zohar (Book of Splendor), the main work of Kabbalistic literature.

Levi, R. Isaac of Berdichev (1740-1809). Famous Hasidic Master whose constant use of the expression "Derbarmdiger Gott" (Merciful Lord), who was known as the "Derbarmdiger" for his principles: love of the Lord and love of his fellow man.

Loew, R. Judah ben Bezalel. *See* **Maharal.**

Luria, R. Yitzhak (b. 1534, Jerusalem; d. 1572, Safed). Known as the "Ari," the "Lion" or "Ari Hakodesh", the Holy Lion, founder of the Lurianic system of Kabbalah.

Luzzatto, R. Moshe Hayim (b. 1707, Padua; d. 1746, Tiberias). Also known by the acronym "RAMHAL." Kabbalist and poet, author of the book, "The One Hundred Thirty Eight Openings to the Kabbalah," and his ethical religious work, Mesillat Yesharim ("Paths of the Upright").

Maharal, Loew, R. Judah ben Bezalel (1525–1609). The Great Rabbi Loew, abbreviated as "MaHaRaL", had earned a reputation as a performer of miracles and famed for his Kabbalistic writings: "Beer ha-Golah," "Netivot Olam," and "Tiferet Israel." It is said he made his famous "Golem" with the knowledge of magic aquired in the book Sefer Yetzira, (see Abraham-Patriarch).

Menahem Azariah of Fano (c. 1609). Famous Italian Kabbalist whose work "Ma'amar ha-Nefesh" follows the mystical idea developed by R. Yitzchak Luria concerning the soul, in that each letter of the Torah represents the upper root of the soul of each individual in Israel. Consequently, each individual soul has its own framework of reference in understanding the Torah.

Moses, R. ben Solomon of Burgos (c. 1230-1300). A leading Kabbalist in Spain, student of Jacob ben Jacob ha-Kohen of Provence.

Nahmanides (b. 1195, Gerona; d. 1270, Akko). R. Moses ben Nahman; abbreviated RaMBAN. Famed Spanish Kabbalist, Talmudic scholar and biblical exegete who adopted a mystical position in the battle which raged around philosophy during the thirteenth century. His commentary on the Sefer Yetzira provides an in-depth comprehension to this abstruse and difficult work on the Kabbalah. His commentary on the Bible cannot be understood apart from a comprehension of the Kabbalah. His opposition to Aristotelianism, which had endangered the very foundations of Judaism in Spain, was completely based on the principal doctrines of the Zohar, which legend relates was already known to Nahmanides. The mysteries of the Kabbalah which initially took hold during the latter half of the twelfth century in Provence and subsequently came to full bloom there and in Northern Spain in the thirteenth century was the Creator's beneficience for a reawakening and rebirth of a new life under its influence. Nahmanides played no small role in this new development if not possibly the harbinger of this movement which climaxed a period in the history of the Jews on which they have always looked back with pride when referring to this "Golden Age in Spain".

Najara, R. Moses (c. 16th century). Kabbalist who lived in Safed and studied within the school of the Lurianic system. Author of several works on the Kabbalah.

Nathan ha-Babli, R. (c.170 c.e.). An older contemporary of R. Judah ha-Nasi of the Talmudic period, author of a parallel work to the Tractate Ethics of the Fathers which is a homiletical exposition of Abot of the Fathers.

Nehemia ben Hakanah, R. (c. 70–130 c.e.). A student of R. Johanan ben Zakkai (Baba Batra 10a). A famed mystic and author of "Ana B'Koah" a recitation included in the morning proyer. This profound mystical prayer is connected with and related to the Seven Sefirot in as much as each of the seven sentences relate to a particular Sefirah. This prayer is also included in the counting of the Omer with its significance being the mystical relationship to each day of the forty-nine days that commence with the second day of Passover and end the day before Shevuot. Since the cosmological influence during this period is considered to be totally negative and destructive, the Ari, R. Isaac Luria, explains in his "Book of Meditation", the use of this prayer in altering the Cosmic influence of these forty-nine days. He has also been considered the author of the famed Kabbalistic text, the "Sefir Bahir."

Rashi-Solomon ben Isaac (Troyes, France 1040-1105). Leading commentator of the Bible and Talmud, and astronomer. Books: Sefer Ha Pardes (Constantinople 1807), Sefer Ha Orah (ed. by S. Buber 1905), Siddur Rashi (S. Bubber 1911), Mahzor Vitry (ed. by S. Hurowitz 1923), Likutey Ha Pardes (Venice 1519), Sefer Issur-Vehetter (printed c. 1925) and more.

Rabad (Poquieres, c. 1125-1198). R. Abraham ben David; known by his acronym "RABD". Kabbalistic and Talmudic authority who lived in Provence. A distinguished authoritative scholar known for his in-depth criticism of Maimonides, produced numerous literary works, Torat ha-Bayit and Ba-al Hanefesh to mention a few. His commentary on the Sefer Yetzirah is of special significance, in as much as this work established the Rabad as one of the most prominent figures in Kabbalistic literature. This work (and his probing into the metaphysical strata of Kabbalah) exerted considerable influence on subsequent Spanish Kabbalists. He defined hertofore abstract concepts with a maximum of clarity. For this he attained for himself a special place in history as one of the greatest commentators on the Kabbalah.

Radbaz. *See* **Zimra, David ben RaDBaZ.**

Rashba. *See* **Aderet, Solomon ben Abraham.**

Recanati, R. Menahem ben Benyamin (c. 1350–1440). Italian Kabbalist, whose family originally came from Spain. His main Kabbalistic work was Perush ol ha-Torah (commentary on the Torah), and Ta'amai ha-Mitzvot (explanation of the precepts). He is quoted extensively throughout the writings of the Ari, R. Isaac Luria. The Ari, mentioning "The Sefer ha-Recanati", tells of an incident where a person, who, on the night of Hoshana Rabba—which according to the Zohar, is the time when we can know if our sins have been purified and we shall live for another year—went out at midnight according to the teachings of the Ari. Upon seeing that his full shadow didn't appear and the head was missing, he knew this was a sign that he needed to attain a higher degree of purity. He returned to the house of study and wept and repented wholeheartedly and when he felt cleaner inside he went outside again and observed that his prayers had been accepted as he saw his full shadow by the light of the moon. (*Gate of Meditation*, p. 307b.)

Saadia ben Joseph Gaon (882–942). Born in Egypt, author, scholar, Kabbalist of the gaonic period and leader of Babylonian Jewry. His original commentary on the Sefer Yetzirah was written in Arabic and translated into Hebrew. His principal work was "Emunot ve-Daot" (Doctrines and opinions).

Saba, Abraham ben Jacob (c. 1500). Spanish Kabbalist and exegete, who settled in Portugal after the expulsion of the Jews from Spain. When forced conversion of Jews was decreed in Portugal in 1497 he left for Fez in Morocco. Known for his famed work on the Bible "Zeror ha-Mor", and "Perush Eser-Sefirot" (Explanation of the Ten Sefirot).

Sahula, Isaac ben Solomon Abi (c. 1240). Scholar and Kabbalist who lived in the town of Guadalajara in Castile. Was a student of the famed

Kabbalist Moses of Burgos and acquaintance of Moses ben Shem Tov de Leon.

Sahula, Meir ben Solomon Abi (c. 1250–1335). Spanish Kabbalist and younger brother of Isaac Abe Sahula who lived in Guadalajara which was then a centre of Kabbalistic learning. Famous for his commentary of the "Sefer Yetzirah" and "Sefer ha-Bahir."

Samuel Vital (c. 1598–1678). Kabbalist, son of Hayim Vital, considered among the important Talmudic authorities of Damascus, re-edited his fathers writings which the Ari, R. Isaac Luria transmitted orally.

Sefer ha-Bahir. *See* **Bahir.**

Sharabi, Shalom (1720–1777). Kabbalist born in Yemen, emigrated to Palestine and studied at the Kabbalistic yeshivah Bet El in Jerusalem. As a Jerusalem Kabbalist, he studied the Lurianic system of Kabbalah; his works are on Lurianic Kabbalah. Particularly famous is his Nehar Shalom, which includes the secrets and meditations on prayer and mitzvot.

Zacuto Abraham ben Samuel (Castille, 1452–c. 1515). Astronomer and historian his parents were French exiles who came to Castille in 1306. Was instructed in his biblical and Talmudical studies by his father Rabi Isaac Aboab, (see Aboab, Isaac). He specialized in Astronomy and Astrology at the University of Salamanca — subsequently becoming a teacher of this field. His major astronomical work is Ha-Hibbur Hagadol (1473–78) a book on the influence of the stars, "Tratado breve en las influencias del cielo" to which he appended a treatise on solar and lunar eclipses: "De las eclipses del sol y de la luna" originally written in Hebrew and later translated into Spanish. When the Jews were expelled from Spain he emigrated to Portugal where he was appointed court astronomer of King John II. In 1504 in Tunis he completed Sefer Hajuhasem. His achievements in astronomy were many. His astrotable of copper enabled the sailors to determine the position of the sun with greater precision. His improved astronomical tables enabled sailors to ascertain latitudes without resource of the meridian of the sun, and to calculate solar and lunar eclipses with greater accuracy.

Zacuto, Moses ben Mordecai (c. 1620–1697). Kabbalist and poet. He was born into a Portuuese Marrano family in Amsterdam. Zacuto published exoteric works in addition to his numerous writings on the Kabbalah.

Zemah, Jacob ben Hayim. Famed 17th century Kabbalist, born in Portugal, settled in Safed where he took up the study of Kabbalah in the Lurianic tradition. Author of many works on the Zohar as well as Lurianic concepts and customs.

Zimra, David ben RaDBaZ (b. 1479, Spain; d. 1573, Safed). Exiled from Spain at age 13, and moved to Safed. In 1512 went to Egypt, where he became spiritual leader until 1569 when he returned to Safed. His distinguished student during his stay in Egypt was the ARi, R. Isaac Luria.

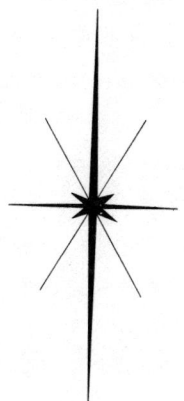

Index

About the Research Centre of Kabbalah

Kabbalah is mystical Judaism. It is the deepest and most hidden meaning of the *Torah*, or Bible. Through the ultimate knowledge and mystical practices of Kabbalah, one can reach the highest spiritual levels attainable. Although many people rely on belief, faith, and dogmas in pursuing the meaning of life, the unknown and the unseen, Kabbalists seek a spiritual connection with the Creator and the forces of the Creator, so that the strange becomes familiar, and faith becomes knowledge.

Throught history, those who knew and practiced the Kabbalah were extremely careful in their dissemination of the knowledge — for they knew the masses of mankind had not yet prepared for the ultimate truth of existance. Today Kabbalists know, through Kabbalistic knowledge, that it is not only proper but necessary to make available the Kabbalah to all who seek it.

The Research Centre of Kabbalah is an independent, non-profit institute founded in Israel in 1922. The Centre provides research, information, and assistance to those who seek the insights of Kabbalah. The Centre offers public lectures, classes, seminars, and excursions to mystical sites at branches in Israel — in Jerusalem, Tel Aviv, Haifa, Beer Sheva, Ashdod, and Ashkelon — and in the United States in New York and Los Angeles. Branches should soon be opened in Mexico City, Buenos Aires, Toronto, and Paris. Thousands of people have benefited by the Centre's activities, and the Centre's publishing of Kabbalistic material continues to be the most comprehensive of its kind in the world including translations in English, Hebrew, Italian, French, Russian, and Spanish.

Kabbalah can provide one with the true meaning of their being and the knowledge necessary for their ultimate benefit. It can show one spirituality which is beyond belief. The Research Centre of Kabbalah will continue to make available the Kabbalah to all those who seek it.

For additional information on the Centre, please contact (in the United States) Research Centre of Kabbalah International, 200 Park Avenue, Suite 303E, New York, N.Y. 10017; telephone (212) 986-2515 or (718) 805-9122.

"Love your fellowman as yourself."

According to the Kabbalah the universe resides in a system where an effect is a result of a cause which is indirect, but is neither random nor accidental. The root of this causality is imbedded in the creation and constitutes a passage to the physical realsm. Within the chain of "cause and effect" is found the life of man, and everything which happens in it. If man will see and understand this chain, he will know how to direct his life towards his goal through the easiest and best path, and will know to implement in a balanced way the love of his fellowman, as it is written, "Love your fellowman as yourself."

> ...[A]nd after forty days that the column will rise from the earth to the heavens in front of the eyes of the whole world the Mashiach will be revealed. From the East side a star will shine in surround this star and will make war with it from all the sides, three times a day for seventy days. And all the people of the world will see....
>
> — *Zohar,* 'Shemot' part 101

The Wisdom of Kabbalah and the Age of Aquarius

The wisdom of Kabbalah dates from thousands of years ago and has accompanied the world since its creation. The sages of Kabbalah have used its hidden knowledge in order to analyze and understand the reason for the universe and the reason for life. Today, in the age of Aquarius, the age of revelations and discoveries, this wisdom is being revealed to the public at large. The wisdom of Kabbalah, which is of "the ancient days", comes to develop whatever is found beyond the five senses of man, and reveals the tremendous forces which are hidden within him. It enlightens the miraculous harmony which exists in the universe and in our world, and directs each person to the harmonious path which is within his own life, and to the harmony which exists between himself and his fellowman.

The Answer to the Essence of Life

Kabbalah is the hidden knowledge of Judaism. Kabbalah sees in Judaism an expression of absolute perfection of the universe, not by way of simply relating to the writings of Judaism in their external sense, but by penetrating to the very depth of truth. With the guidance of the book of Zohar written by Rabbi Shimon bar Yochai, it becomes possible for us to reach the essence of things, understand their roots, and directly reveal the solution to problems. Usually man relates to life within the framework of effects and results which are a collection of secondary branches, and which impede man's more basic, primary vision of the complete chain of events. The Kabbalah teaches us to see how the bridges are built between that which is in the Zohar concerning the past, present, and future, and the bridges upon which we have arrived today. The book of Zohar, with an intense light, illuminates the path which leads to the true solution of any problem from the most simple to the most complex.

"There is no question in the universe to which you will not find an answer in the teachings of Kabbalah," Rabbi Dr. P.S. Berg.

Courses Offered in the Research Centre of Kabbalah

It is the privilege of every man to reach the most elevated heights of understanding himself and the universe around him. The way to this understanding is through the teachings of Kabbalah. The Research Centre of Kabbalah presents courses in various fields of Kabbalah and studies in different levels of Zohar ranging from beginners to advanced levels. The following is a list of courses offered in the Research Centre of Kabbalah with a brief description of each course.

•*Kabbalah Basic Course*
This course includes the definition of terms and an introduction of understanding the principles of Kabbalah. It also includes concepts which are in effect the primary keys to the teaching of mysticism. This course represents an indispensable basis for the rest of the subjects which are taught in the Centre, even to the most advanced levels of Kabbalah studies.

•*Kabbalistic Meditation*
Kabbalistic meditation is a method of self-reflection dating from ancient days. It is based on the method of the previous Kabbalists and

has been unified and simplified by the saintly ARI, Rabbi Yitzhak Luria, one of the great Kabbalists of Safed. This is a practical method which brings us to high levels of awareness and to the true evaluation of the forces which are hidden in man. Kabbalistic meditation acquires for us the tools necessary for bridging the gap between the forces of the soul and the forces of the body, and brings us to a growing utilization of the potential that is imbedded in us.

•Reincarnation and Life After Death

The Kabbalah sees in life not only a process of birth and death, but a continuous chain of cycles in which the soul (the inner energy of man) enters this world to fulfill a particular duty, and "leaves" it several times. The soul returns to the process of life many times in different bodies, up to the point where she reaches a perfect completion of the duty which has been assigned to her.

The understanding of this process leads to the understanding of all the processes which take place in the life of man. During his lifetime a man may ask himself who he is, why he was born to particular parents in a particular neighborhood; he is called by a name that was "fixed" for him and finds himself in a particular society to fulfill a particular duty. Why does he meet a particular spouse to bring into the world children with particular personalities and the like? There awaits to be revealed an amazing composition of a picture of a puzzle which when seen explains to us every instant of our lives, and also explains the historical process of life and the world, from its creation to its completion.